ABOLITION:
OVERCOMING
THE CHRISTIAN ESTABLISHMENT
ON EDUCATION

DEDICATION

This book is dedicated to my daughter Reagan Elizabeth, over whose mind the civil government has no jurisdiction; and to my wife Corinne, whose obedience to God and faith in me, have allowed me to declare that to be the truth.

ABOLITION: OVERCOMING THE CHRISTIAN ESTABLISHMENT ON EDUCATION

KEVIN R. NOVAK, ESQ.

DECONSTRUCTING THE COLISEUM, LLC
LYNCHBURG, VA

Publisher:
Deconstructing the Coliseum, LLC
P.O. Box 1115
Forest, VA 24551

BOOK COVER DESIGN BY CORY BLACK, CREATION MESSAGE

ISBN 978-0-9980788-0-9

CONTENTS

INTRODUCTION

This book is about civil government school system abolition. The flesh invades me from time to time, so I fantasize about receiving accolades awarded to the most sophisticated, articulate, and earth-shattering author for one's time. Almost simultaneously, I cringe about humanists and Christians throwing bricks through my window. Either way I would appreciate the attention given to the civil government school system abolition issue, as it would be a step in the right direction, and as I agree there is no such thing as bad publicity.

As I pondered writing this book, I knew the issue deserved this attention-gathering mechanism, yet it is such a long process, and while I am not afraid of work, I was just not sure that anything else could be said on the abolition issue: humanism[1] has been addressed; the physical and spiritual swords have been contrasted; and the biblical/legal arguments have been made.[2] What is left but to perpetuate those ideas? A book, especially in today's media environment, is not always needed to do this.

Periodically, though, it does become necessary to repeat and republish those things already said

---

[1] I adopt Cornelius Van Til's *humanism* definition: "[T]he view that man is the highest value and authority in ethics and knowledge, which makes it functionally equivalent to 'autonomy.'" Greg L. Bahnsen, *Van Til's Apologetic*, (Phillipsburg, NJ: P & R Publishing, 1998), 111.

[2] When I write "legal" here I mean God's revealed law, not man's arbitrary positive law.

clearly and precisely. From time to time it is good practice to assert things in a slightly different manner; and from time to time the tree of liberty must be refreshed with Jesus' blood. All those reasons are enough to compel one to readdress an issue. Moreover, I am honest and humble when I write that I do have some things to tell you–things that have not yet been said and things that must be said. This book is not just about abolition but also about American[3] Christendom's leaders. God's Word does not justify the civil government school system's existence, yet American Christendom's leaders disengage that very issue and, consequently, we incur God's curses, which hinder the gospel. American Christendom's leaders, whom I label the "Christian Establishment," do not espouse how the Bible does not justify a civil government school's existence, and that failure disengages the humanist's church: the civil government school system. That disengagement directly causes fewer humans to hear the gospel. Posterity must know how the Christian Establishment has failed.

Many of the things I share with you will be anecdotal, but I think, when extrapolated, hold true. Many are tidbits, subtle observations, and quite honestly, things with which you are likely to disagree with upon first reading. But understand that in sharing with you here, I do so in obedience to God, not because this is something I want to do. Almost a decade ago I was sitting in my State Farm

---

[3] In this work any reference to America means the United States of America.

2

cubicle, making a very comfortable living doing something that was very easy for me. My wife and I were on pace for very early retirement. I am not trying to sound melodramatic, as if worthy of martyrdom, but I could have stuck to disobedience and comfort. Instead, I chose the opposite: obedience and discomfort. Nonetheless, what qualifies as comfort is not necessarily dispositive as to what is proper; God's Word is dispositive as to what is proper. The bottom line is that, despite how your preacher will warn you about this book, you need to take a long, hard look at what I share with you here. If you do, you will be so much better spiritually, and if enough congregations read this, God's Holy Ghost may spark a revival.

I was in my third and final law school year when I discovered the late Greg L. Bahnsen's audio series, *Defending the Christian Worldview Against All Opposition*.[4] I had yet to put together the theological puzzle pieces, so I was open to Bahnsen, whose audio series and its accompanying posthumously published book, *Always Ready*, took me from the shallow Christianity preachers present, to Christian depth that is not arbitrarily limited to personal morality, so repugnant to American Christendom. Bahnsen was the first in a series of non-canon humans God utilized to provoke me into a personal great awakening–one that I think is still

---

[4] Bahnsen, *Defending the Christian Worldview against All Opposition: Series One: Weapons of Our Spiritual Warfare; Series Two: Destroying All Speculations* (Powder Springs, GA: American Vision, 2010). Sound recording.

ongoing, and one that I think was a result of finally realizing that a failure to question the civil government school's existence is America's problem.

Eventually I came to understand there are different reasons the Christian Establishment refuses to address a civil government school's existence. Some in the Christian Establishment are in the Romans 13 negligence crowd: Christian leaders who refuse to espouse that the civil government has limits, and those limits preclude the civil government operating schools. Some in the Christian Establishment are in the end times speculation crowd: Christian leaders who think that, because Jesus is coming back, we should not waste resources on externalizing Christianity for the sake of Christian infrastructure. Some in the Christian Establishment are in the Christian freedom crowd: Christian leaders who frame American education as being a function of delegation rather than jurisdiction. Some in the Christian Establishment are in the Lord Jesus disobedience crowd: Christian leaders who espouse that obedience to Jesus (as a function of salvation) means merely evangelizing that Jesus is the Savior, and Christian leaders who reduce Lord Jesus obedience to mere personal morality. Because the Christian Establishment disengages how there are civil government schools, America continually incurs God's curses. Those curses hinder the gospel. The Christian Establishment is gatekeeping the gospel, and possibly an American revival.

In this book I do not judge another's salvation. I deal with sanctification and, in doing so, one's *external manifestations* as a function of his regeneration (or lack thereof). A person's external manifestations are going to inform me about the person's regeneration (or again, lack thereof), or what could be called "heart" concepts in Deuteronomy 7:17, Deuteronomy 8:5, Psalms 19:14, Romans 1:21, and Romans 10:10. Obviously I am unable to see a person's heart, so I must judge external manifestations.

Further, there is judging a person's external manifestations relative to societal norms, and there is judging a person's external manifestations relative to civil law. In other words, there is judging a person's external manifestations to determine whether to let him into your home,[5] and there is judging a person's external manifestations to determine whether to put him to death.[6] The former is commanded; so is the latter, but only to the civil magistrate. All this is to say that, in this text, I do not analyze whether one is regenerated; rather, I analyze one's external manifestations.

Excitingly, this book presents concepts with which you are probably not familiar. I first present how God's Word does not justify the civil government school system's existence. That presentation begins with *ultimate authority*, which dovetails into

---

[5] 2 John 1:10.
[6] Leviticus 20:9.

jurisdiction, and develops into *Romans 13*. I then present how, through the ideologies above, the Christian Establishment disengages the humanist's church: the civil government school system. Subsequently, I elaborate on how that disengagement causes curses on America, hindering the gospel. Lastly, in wanting to be part of the solution and not just diagnosing the problem, I discuss Christian education policy and how we break that negative cycle via God's Holy Ghost.

I pause to define "Christian Establishment": American Christendom's leaders, led mainly by Christian attorneys, preachers, and pro-family organizations, who refuse to address, debate, and discuss whether there should be a civil government school system. The "Christian Establishment" is different than "American Christendom." The latter is the larger American body (mainly congregations) of confessed believers; the former is American Christendom's leaders.

As I stated above I pondered whether to write this book, to some degree maybe due to the fear that I may not properly articulate these issues. After all, these issues are very clear to me but hard to quantify, and at the same time, most likely amorphous to you. I make observations about human behavior in the aggregate, which, in order for you to see what I see, will require your time and effort. What we address together as author and reader is not something that can be touched and physically analyzed. It is abstract, fluid, yet still real, and it takes time to fully understand these matters. At my best I guide you through these tenets, with which I am confident you will eventually agree, if given the opportunity, outside your pastor's purview specifically and the Christian Establishment generally. Further, what I address is a function of years of experience with, and observation of, the Christian Establishment, and in bringing these words to you, my goal–I firmly emphasize–is not to divide but to galvanize. John MacArthur states in the Preface to his book *The Gospel According to Jesus,* that on the Lordship Salvation issue (on which he wrote) he "prayed" and "diligently sought the Lord's guidance," hoping to provoke discussion.[7] Likewise, I prayed and sought the Lord's guidance. I hope this book provokes discussion.

Finally, I am not short on answers, yet in this book I tend to ask rhetorical questions. That is not an indication that I do not know, nor that I am a skeptic; I think, in fact, we can *know*, as God has revealed sufficient knowledge to us for everyday life. But our fallible perspective and fleshly desires so oftentimes hinder us from understanding God's Revelation. With other Christians we must actively explore what God has revealed, even if–maybe especially if–some label those matters "controversial." What the Christian Establishment labels "controversial" may just be the very iron sharpening iron we so badly need in America.

---

[7] John F. MacArthur, Jr., *The Gospel According to Jesus.* (Grand Rapids: Zondervan, 1988), XV.

Your preacher may warn you about this book. If so, understand that that is *the* exact thing causing America's decline: a refusal to unleash God's Holy Spirit on us so we can be further sanctified as a body of believers, breaking the negative cycle the Christian Establishment has us in.

CHAPTER 1
GOD'S WORD DOES NOT JUSTIFY THE CIVIL GOVERNMENT SCHOOL SYSTEM'S EXISTENCE

ULTIMATE AUTHORITY

On more than one occasion a pastor has prompted me to provide input on the law, as I am an attorney. I am always confounded, as I wonder if those pastors really believe that Scripture is the starting point to everything in God's Creation, including law. Particularly, *Why is a pastor, who is supposed to be an expert in handling Scripture, asking a congregant what the law is?* He has access to the same data to which I have access: Scripture. In that regard, I do my best not to make the same mistake. Thus, when someone asks me a question about law, I respond in the most sophisticated way possible. First, *What do the Scriptures say?*, and second, *How do you read them?* Those two questions[8] should frame the Christian's approach to everything, including law. The first question speaks to how Scripture is the starting point for knowing something; the second question speaks to understanding the Scriptures. Therefore, for the Christian, no matter how he defines law, the starting point must be Scripture.

---

[8] Luke 10:26.

9

You may deem it overly philosophical to converse about law; I do not. I think law is a function of ultimate authority, and I revel in such thoughts. Nonetheless, a human unilaterally labeling something "philosophical" does not make it so; nor does labeling something "philosophical" make something irrelevant. Likewise, unilaterally labeling something "religious" does not make it so, or irrelevant. It just means that, if you fail to deal with what you deem philosophical or religious, you are suppressing the truth. Thus, you are not off the hook since philosophy means something: the study of epistemology (one's source of knowledge), ethics (personal morality, societal norms, and civil law), and metaphysics (nature of reality). There is no need to elaborate on those terms here, because each of those terms means something quantified by other terms. Here, it is only necessary that, after all that analysis, we are back to the very thing we should comport our lives to: Scripture. And in that regard, *What do the Scriptures say?*, and *How do you read them?*

No matter your definition of "law," a law is a principle. And to determine life's principles and how they apply we must start with Scripture. Further, there are different types of principles, which invokes additional analysis about which ones apply merely to the individual (personal morality) or to society as a whole (societal norms and civil law). I thoroughly enjoy contemplating what principles should comprise all types of law, including civil law. I also thoroughly enjoy contemplating how those principles are supposed to reflect God's biblical principles, and how what we do on an everyday basis correlates negatively or positively with biblical principles. Even as a starting point it is exciting (and sometimes frustrating) deciphering which parts of Scripture are principles and which are historical facts. Then, of those historical facts, which should we emulate?

It is sometimes difficult to determine which historical persons documented in Scripture, other than Jesus Christ, we should emulate. When encountered with the issue as to whether to emulate a biblical figure there is risk of confusing an "is" with a "should," meaning just because a person did something, that does not mean we should do it. My fallibility is on full display when I admit that it is not always clear to me when I should emulate a person documented in Scripture. That includes Jesus: I am not sure it would be wise for me to encounter and evangelize the Samaritan woman at the well, as did Jesus.[9] But this is why Jesus is known as the universe's governing principle (or presupposition), as his facts are principles we should pursue and emulate.[10] Someday I may evangelize the Samaritan woman at the well if my heart becomes more like Jesus' heart.

I do not think these are overly philosophical issues; I think they are wholly relevant to everyday life. More than that, what you have never discussed in

---

[9] John 4:1-26.
[10] There are some exceptions.

Sunday school or Wednesday night class is that questions of facts and principles are wholly relevant to civil government. I understand that not everybody unpacks principles the same way; that is because of fallible man, not a God whose Revelation is unclear. It is my own fallibility that leads me to cling to what, in apologetics, is called "presuppositionalism." Essentially, all I have to offer is, *What do the Scriptures say?* and *How should I read them?* My starting point is Scripture because I have no other answers to offer you.

Even if you reject *biblical* principles, which are Jesus-centered, you still attach and anchor your principles to some source. Thus, for every human, principles relating to personal morality, societal norms, and civil law come from an ultimate source– an *ultimate authority*. Any principle in existence is going to reflect, to some degree, either impliedly or expressly, one's ultimate authority. And an ultimate authority is always a person. When you cite a principle, it is a function of who you assume is the ultimate authority out of the category of persons. So the proper inquiry is not, *Do you have an ultimate authority?* Nor is it, *What is your ultimate authority?* Rather, it is, *Who is your ultimate authority?* The Christian designates Jesus as the ultimate authority; the non-Christian designates someone else. Jesus is the bread of life, the wellspring of eternal life, the beginning and end through whom all things were made, the source of all knowledge and wisdom. That is, Jesus is the Word and, therefore, the Scriptures.

The fact that your ultimate authority is a person and not a thing directly confronts the notion that, in the United States, the U.S. Constitution is the ultimate authority. In like manner, it confronts the notion that the U.S. Constitution speaks law and is then the source of law. The Christian's mistake is starting with the U.S. Constitution as the ultimate authority, thinking it should be cited as the final arbiter on legal decisions. The U.S. Constitution is, after all, merely comprised of words written on paper; for that matter so is Scripture. But the U.S. Constitution is not God-breathed, and so the reason the Christian makes a mistake in starting with the U.S. Constitution over Scripture is that he is conceding his ultimate authority is man and not God. On the public policy level it means he is starting public negotiations by conceding half of his territory. The humanist makes no such mistake, and that is why our public policy tends to be humanistic.

Regarding how your ultimate authority is a person, consider how the U.S. Constitution must be interpreted: It is humans who declare what the words mean. When I was in law school, I was told that a court of law is an "it." I adamantly oppose that characterization. Courts are comprised of humans: judges are human, jurors are human, and if you can believe it, attorneys are human. The Supreme Court of the United States is comprised of humans, each of whom has an ultimate authority. Granted, they do not all adopt the same ultimate authority; their decisions are an amalgam (accounting for split decisions and different rationales). Nevertheless, there are nine judges on the Supreme Court of the United States, and each designates an ultimate authority. Not incidentally, they all think like humanists, as each rejects Jesus as the anchor to civil law.

In further regards to how your ultimate authority is a person, consider how, when the Framers were writing the U.S. Constitution, they had to cite someone else. That is why the U.S. Constitution is not the ultimate authority. To say otherwise–and this iterates the Christian's mistake–is to regard the Framers as the ultimate authorities. A Framer should not be considered the ultimate authority though, nor should the Framers as an amalgam be considered the ultimate authority, because (as I just asserted) when they were writing the U.S. Constitution, they were each citing someone else. Granted, it is true one could argue that the Framers were, when writing the U.S. Constitution, anchoring to and then elaborating on the Declaration of Independence. With that, I do not disagree. Nevertheless, that merely shifts the discussion to *whom* the Framers were invoking when they wrote the Declaration of Independence. Christians then who cite the Framers as justification for what public policy should be, are engaging in at least quasi-humanist reasoning, since the Christian's line of reasoning must ultimately be anchored to Jesus, not another human, including any Framer. Not incidentally, I think the Framers would agree with me here; they thought Jesus is the ultimate authority.

The mistake of citing the Framers for justification of what *should* be is hopefully made clear by citing the so-called separation of church and state. This debate is not new to America; it goes back centuries. Generally, the Christian's line of reasoning centers on the U.S. Constitution's First Amendment and how "Congress shall make no law respecting an establishment of religion...."[11] That is, the Christian will generally argue that *state* civil governments may make a law respecting establishment of Christianity, as the Establishment Clause prohibits only *Congress* from doing so. But I quite easily blow a hole in that interpretation. As I elaborate on below, Romans 13 precludes civil governments from operating a systematic religion, or church, on any level. *The proper Christian perspective is that the combined local, state, and federal civil government actions may not exceed civil government actions permitted in Romans 13.* Scripture does not justify using force and coercion to advance thought on any level. That same reasoning applies to the U.S. Constitution's Tenth Amendment, which reserves powers to the States (or the people). Just because the power[12] to operate a systematic religion is not enumerated to the *federal* civil government, it does not mean a *state* or

---

[11] *U.S. Constitution.* Amend. I.

[12] Just as *politics* and *civil government* are not synonymous, *power* and *authority* are not synonymous. But generally I use those terms interchangeably in this book.

local civil government may use force and coercion in that manner, for the same reason: Romans 13.

An Establishment Clause, when properly viewed from the Christian perspective, means this: within a system of civil government that is divided into local, state, and federal levels, no level shall go beyond what Romans 13 permits. And Romans 13 limits the civil government to promoting good and punishing evildoers. Yet sadly, in (supposedly) relying on the Framers, many Christians argue that it is proper for there to be established religions on the state civil government level, but not the federal civil government level, because of how only Congress is theoretically prohibited via the Establishment Clause or because of the Tenth Amendment. But that is the wrong line of reasoning, based on the wrong ultimate authority, even if the Framers said (or acted) otherwise. To iterate, combined local, state, and federal civil governments cannot exceed what Romans 13 permits. In other words, just because the First Amendment or Tenth Amendment impliedly holds that state (or local) civil government actors may make a law respecting an establishment of religion, that does not make it proper. Scripture is what determines propriety–or, in the case of a civil government-established religion, impropriety. It is not the Framers' documents that are ultimate, it is Jesus' Scriptures.

Still regarding the relationship between church and state, or otherwise labeled the distinction between church government and civil government, Christians and humanists alike enjoy citing Thomas Jefferson's letter to the Danbury Baptists.[13] Yet, when writing his letter, Jefferson must have had someone else informing him about what *should* be, and, thus what to write. So discussions pertaining to the Establishment Clause's terms "law," "establishment," and "religion" can be had–that is fine; but if one assumes Jefferson's letter to the Danbury Baptists, or any other Framer writing, is dispositive of the relationship between church government and civil government, that is eliminating *the* proper someone else that should have been relied upon when President Jefferson wrote the letter. This is really to say that if you rely on Jefferson, as does our nation's Supreme Court, to dictate where to draw the line between church government and civil government, then Jefferson is the ultimate authority on the matter. That obviously precludes Scripture from being the ultimate authority on the matter.

It is not harmless error to rely on the Framers to the exclusion of Scripture. That is because it is asking, *What do the Framers say?* and *How do you read them?*, relying on them as the ultimate authority. The concept I present to you here is that, from the Christian's perspective, it is unwise for Jefferson's

---

[13] *See* Daniel Dreisbach *Thomas Jefferson and the Wall of Separation between Church and State* (New York: NYU Press, 2002). Dreisbach's book is an excellent source on the matter; I do think though that the Bible (mainly here Romans 13) should be the source of all jurisprudence.

Danbury Baptist letter to be the ultimate authority on where to draw the line between church government and civil government, because that is then done in disregard to Scripture. Not to mention that Jefferson's letter to the Danbury Baptists is not ultimate, as it does not claim to be. All ultimate authorities are self-authenticating. Nevertheless, if you as a Christian want to reason from Jefferson as the self-authenticating ultimate authority and starting point, especially as it relates to church government and civil government, you have just adopted an ultimate authority other than Jesus. That makes you either a humanist or a Christian who thinks like one.

As a sidebar, I insert here how I am not against those who argue that writings are important to our society. Constitutional attorney and scholar Herb Titus has emphasized through many media that the stellar Chief Justice John Marshall outlined in *Marbury v. Madison* how our U.S. Constitution "is written," connoting a resemblance to our Lord Jesus' repeated responses[14] to Satan's temptations. The Western Legal Tradition emphasizes writings as a way to make meaning static and a way to hedge against tyranny. I agree with all that, as with the Rule of Law, which emphasizes that there is a law external to ourselves. While that is true, we have to go to the correct ultimate authority for that law. It is worth repeating that, when we invoke ultimate authority, we must invoke the correct writings: Scripture.

---

[14] Matthew 4:4.

The Bible is what informs all of humanity about the distinction between church government and civil government. And while our application of that distinction is at times fuzzy, it does not negate the fact that if there is no Jehovah, then the Bible is just another set of man-made constructs that may be overruled and disregarded. Humanism, (the lie that man is the measure of all things, the lawgiver, and the ultimate authority) negates itself. That is, if there is no Jehovah, then there is no such church government and civil government distinction. If man is the source of law and the final arbiter of truth, that opens the door to *every* man being the source of law and the final arbiter of truth (autonomy). If every man is the source of law, it follows that every man's laws are equally valid (relativism). Thus anyone can espouse a different church-state distinction, forcing a tie between distinctions and humans; in accord with itself, humanism cannot prevail under that scenario; therefore, it cannot prevail against Christianity.

For the Christian to disregard Scripture when analyzing church government and civil government, or anything else for that matter, is to disregard the only basis he has. After all, if there are eight billion ultimate authorities roaming the planet, then life becomes a public, physical power struggle. Oftentimes when confronted with that dilemma, and relying on his own supposed sophistication or self-restraint, the humanist denies that he thinks life should be demoted to such a thing as a public, physical power struggle, as if his bow tie precludes such a mentality. But it is not a straw man argument to say that without Jehovah there is no law, liberty, justice, or church government and civil government distinction. It is *pushing the antithesis*; it is showing the fool his folly, which Scripture commands us to do.[15]

The Christian must (first) assume Scripture is the source of ultimate authority, and (second) reason from that source. The Christian must be a *biblical presuppositionalist*, not a *Framer presuppositionalist*. In practice, that means instead of asking, *What do the Framers say?*, it is asking, *What do the Scriptures say?* Biblical presuppositionalism is the way of articulating defensively and offensively the Christian worldview. It stands against all other apologetics in that it requires the apologist to assume Jehovah's ultimate authority even before using the Scriptures to reason. Biblical presuppositionalism means initially assuming–or presupposing–God's Word prior to any type of biblical worldview application, requiring total biblical faith, commitment, and application to all areas of life. There is no neutral ground in God's universe; thus, the biblical presuppositional apologist cannot tolerate a Framer presuppositional framework for biblical worldview application. That is because the Framer presuppositionalist starts with a man as the ultimate authority, not Jehovah.

---

[15] Proverbs 26:5.

In further unpacking ultimate authority, there is such a thing as "case law." Case law is law that takes the general to the more specific. Recognize how the general body of law labeled "case law" is not necessarily equivalent to that which is labeled "common law." Common law[16] is the traditional English case law that resembles Scripture. It is true that common law is case law, but case law is not always common law.

Case law refines a general principle so that it can apply to a specific situation or *case*. For example, suppose Joe goes out for the evening and his parents tell him, "Be home by ten." The general principle is that Joe must be home by ten. Joe fully understands, but nevertheless he arrives home by ten o'clock–AM. Did Joe comply? The parents give Joe a break after reluctantly admitting their ambiguity. So the next time Joe goes out he is told, "Be home by ten o'clock–PM." Joe fully understands, but this time he arrives home by ten o'clock PM, but with thirty seconds elapsed. Thus, he was home at 10:00:30 PM. Did Joe comply? The parents once again give Joe a break due to their reluctantly admitted ambiguity. So the next time Joe goes out he is told, "Be home by ten o'clock PM, with zero seconds." Joe fully understands, but this time he arrives at ten PM with zero seconds, only he is merely in the driveway and not in the home. Did Joe comply? You see, every time there was an alleged principle violation, a more specific articulation needed to be

---

[16] William Blackstone, *Commentaries on the Laws of England* (Chicago: University of Chicago Press, 1979).

made. Those articulations are *case law*. They serve as precedent for future situations or cases.

While case law affords the opportunity to bring the general to the specific, it does not necessarily mean the specifics are grounded in the correct ultimate authority. In fact, the Supreme Court's case law, which makes more specific the U.S. Constitution, goes directly against God and the biblical principles revealed to us. For example, in taking the U.S. Constitution's Fourteenth Amendment from the general to the specific, the Supreme Court referenced an ultimate authority other than Jehovah in coming to the specific determination that there is a "right" to marry someone of the same sex. That is in direct disregard to Scripture, which cites homosexuality[17] as a sin and marriage between a male and female.[18]

Still further regarding case law, there is case law that unpacks the Ten Commandments, which is an actual body of law, binding on humans. To be sure, it more and more stands in direct contrast to the Supreme Court's case law. Thankfully God gives us case law in Exodus, Leviticus, and Deuteronomy, which I find very helpful, especially when it comes to *intent*. Paradoxically, despite how Christians generally accept as binding the Ten Commandments, they reject the Ten Commandments' specific applications. The case law that unpacks the Ten Commandments is

---

[17] Leviticus 18:22; Romans 1:26-27; 1 Corinthians 6:9.
[18] Matthew 19:3-9.

repugnant to so many Christians. Evidence of this is by way of illustration using another U.S. Constitution provision, the Eighth Amendment,[19] which prohibits cruel and unusual punishment. Ask a Christian if the death penalty for sexual immorality is cruel and unusual punishment, and he will likely answer in the affirmative. Thus, the common Christian considers the death penalty for sexual immorality prohibited under the U.S. Constitution's Eighth Amendment. That is poor reasoning, though, and humanistic.

Whether you think the death penalty for sexual immorality is *currently* binding is separate from whether it ever *was* binding. And whether it *is* currently binding does not determine whether it is cruel and unusual. At one point the death penalty for sexual immorality, you must concede, was binding, even if just for the Israelites. So if you call the God of the Bible's judgment on sexual immorality cruel and unusual, then you are impeaching God. Although you may hold the death penalty for sexual immorality is not currently binding, it is not cruel and unusual, unless of course you deem the God of the Bible to be cruel and unusual.

This case law analysis is simply for showing how principles are brought from the general to the specific, and that human reasoning is anchored to an ultimate authority. Meaning, in taking a general principle to a specific principle, the human (first)

---

[19] *U.S. Constitution.* Amend. VIII.

relies on an ultimate authority and then (second) applies the principles that emanate from that ultimate authority. Those principles correlate, positively or negatively, with Scripture. There is no way around that, which means you either have Jesus as the ultimate authority or you have some other human as the ultimate authority.

If you explore the English common law, you will find that the effort was made there to have that case law correlate positively with biblical principles. Nevertheless, as contemporary Christians begin with the U.S. Constitution when engaging the humanist on legal issues, it is done in vain. That is because the U.S. Constitution is interpreted by humans: when there is a general principle at issue, like one in the U.S. Constitution, human interpreters look to the existing humanistic case law, and then either confirm it or add to it more specificity. In doing so they had to have first adopted an ultimate authority, and currently that ultimate authority is not Jesus; it is some other human. American courts long ago began suppressing Jesus as the ultimate authority.[20]

Now, as I said, without Jehovah, who manifested himself long ago in the temporal realm as Jesus, life becomes a public, physical power struggle. That public, physical power struggle is not always with physical weaponry. Indeed, in our nation, for now,

---

[20] That judges suppress the truth is evidence they know the truth. For them not to allow Jesus in civil government schools they must first assume he is the ultimate authority.

24

the power struggle is through other means. One means is "majoritarianism": the majority wins. But majoritarianism cannot be the ultimate authority, if at one time the majority was ever a (numeric) minority, which undermines the assertion, insofar as when the majority was a minority, they must have relied on someone else to know what should be. That someone else was either Jesus or it was not.

Another means relied upon as a power struggle arbiter is that of *the people*. This, of course, is often cited due to the U.S. Constitution's Preamble, which begins, "We the People." The people's power is justified by way of them as a majority (as in majoritarianism just above), the ballot box, or the legislature. In those forms, the people typically flex their muscles by saying something to the effect of, "We are the people and we are in charge, so our representatives must listen to us!" This seems admirable, and it may very well be; nevertheless, it may be humanistic. You see, *the people* are, in fact, composed of persons, and all persons are ... human. Thus, before one can assert power as *the people*, he or she must have first been informed by someone else. That someone else was Jesus or it was not. That holds true for the ballot box too, as before one casts a ballot, he must have first been informed by someone else. That someone else was Jesus or it was not. Likewise, it holds true for citing the legislature as the final arbiter. The legislature is, in fact, composed of persons–again, all human. And prior to voting on public policy, those humans must have been informed by someone else. That someone else was Jesus or it was not.

The interaction between the people and the legislature highlights a special issue: circular reasoning. If you go to a legislator and ask him to justify his public policy, he will cite the people. Yet if you go to the people to justify that same public policy, they will cite the legislator (or the amalgam legislature). That interaction is telling in that each cites another human, other than Jesus, as his ultimate authority. It may, then, very well be the case that either has yet to experience a Supervening Cause breaking their humanistic circularity. In that respect, there is nothing without circularity, as on a grand scale, all reasoning is circular. But you must rely on the correct circular reasoning: All Scripture is God-breathed. How do we know? Scripture states so.[21]

As best I can help it, my main emphasis when discussing any civil government-related topic is that the civil government is comprised of someone who, when making any decision, first adopts an ultimate authority before he applies that ultimate authority's principles. In other words, when discussing what the civil government should do, it is not a matter of *what*, but rather *who*. Consistently, the same must be concluded when we talk about the family government, which is comprised of *people*. And, of course, the same must be concluded when we talk about the church government, which is comprised

---

[21] 2 Timothy 3:16.

26

of *people*. All governments illustrate how one's ultimate authority is not a piece of paper, but a person. Joshua declared so[22] and so did his forefathers; so should each nation.[23]

It is indeed puzzling why the family is a "they" and the church is a "they," but the civil government is an "it." If knowledge means knowing what God's principles are, and wisdom means knowing how to apply them, then how can a piece of paper have such wisdom? When we look at a constitution, or any other written words, what is not dispositive is whether they are written, but rather whether they conform to the ultimate authority. That ultimate authority is Jesus or it is not.

Again, I have an appreciation for things written. To say otherwise is to contradict the obvious fact that God has revealed to us things that He commanded to be written. The benefit to something written is that it can be contextualized, revisited, and more easily shared. Neil Postman, in *Amusing Ourselves to Death*,[24] wonderfully unpacked all that, and said nothing, especially in citing the still venerable Chief Justice John Marshall, with which I disagree. Despite all that, though, every human can cite a document not in accord with his ultimate authority; that is to say, once again, just because words are

---

[22] Joshua 24:15.
[23] Psalms 33:12; 2 Chronicles 7:14.
[24] Neil Postman, *Amusing Ourselves to Death: Public Discourse in the Age of Show Business* (New York: Penguin Books, 1986).

written on paper does not mean those words are necessarily final. What is dispositive is which ultimate authority is relied upon. Cornelius Van Til wrote this:

> It is our contention that only the Christian can obtain real coherence in his thinking. If all of our thoughts about the facts of the universe are in correspondence with God's ideas of these facts, there will naturally be coherence in our thinking because there is a complete coherence in God's thinking.[25]

The Bible must be the Christian's starting point to all life's areas.

JURISDICTION

The civil government has no right to operate a school system, because the civil government has no jurisdiction over the heart and mind. The term "jurisdiction" is comprised of the prefix "juris," Latin for "law," and the suffix "diction," Latin for "to speak"; thus jurisdiction means "to speak law."

That law is "spoken" does not necessarily mean it is verbalized; rather, it means that law has a source. And because law has a source, it follows that it is

---

[25] Bahnsen, *Van Til's Apologetic: Readings and Analysis* (Phillipsburg, N.J: P & R Publishers, 1998), 169.

bound up with concepts such as ideology, philosophy, worldview, and religion. For God has spoken law to us, as we know from 2 Timothy 3:16, that all Scripture is God-breathed. Know, though, that just because you reject Scripture as your ultimate authority and law source, it does not mean that your assertion of what the law should be does not have a source: everyone has a law source; everyone has an ultimate authority.

A law is merely a principle, and an asserted principle is a proposition, one that is either true or false. Thus speaking law means proposing what is true and false based on an ultimate authority. That is why law and ultimate authority are inextricable; a human cannot propose or enact a law without first assuming and invoking an ultimate authority.

Hopefully this sheds further light on how, when dealing with ultimate authority, one is not dealing with *what*, but rather *who*. A constitution cannot speak, yet humans can, meaning that when we anchor what a constitution means based on humans unpacking that constitution (via man's case law), we are subscribing to humanism to the exclusion of God. Constitutions cannot be the ultimate law source, because when constitutions are written and interpreted, an ultimate authority is first referenced. When the U.S. Constitution was written, the assumed ultimately authority was God (via

Scripture) as invoked in the Declaration of Independence.[26]

Dealing with jurisdiction means dealing with ultimate authority, because only an ultimate authority can speak law. An ultimate authority that speaks law may be you, your Uncle Joe, or Jesus; but nevertheless, it is an ultimate authority that, for you, speaks law. Despite the possibility that an individual or a whole society impliedly or expressly rejects Scripture, Jesus' law is still what governs His Creation.

As jurisdiction means "to speak law," a reference to jurisdiction could theoretically mean a reference to all of Scripture. However, jurisdiction connotes something narrower than all of Scripture. Think of jurisdiction as meaning law over some particular area of life, and the way to assert law over some particular area of life is by performing duties owed to God, also called *rights*. Rights are duties owed to God–*responsibilities*. Scripture is what informs us about what rights we have and what duties we owe God.

The crucial point with rights is where they originate–man or God. In pushing the antithesis, if rights do not come from Jehovah–the transcendent anchor to reality–there are no rights, because that something one may want to perform can be

---

[26] The Declaration of Independence reads, "[All men] are endowed by their Creator with certain unalienable Rights [.]"

physically overcome by one of the political[27] means enumerated above, or by brute physical force. That undermines the very idea of there being the inherent ability to do something, making the "right" alienable. If an asserted "right" is alienable, it is not a right. Put another way, if Jesus were on Earth ruling as the civil magistrate, if in that capacity he considered something you did to be a crime, that crime would not be considered a "right." In conjunction, if right now Jesus considered something you did to be a sin, that sin should never receive a protected status under the civil magistrate.

Each family government, church government, and civil government has duties owed to God. The family government[28] has the duties owed to God to establish marriage, be fruitful and multiply, teach God's commands to children, and discipline children in full submission to Christ. The church government[29] has the duties owed to God to disciple the nations, mediate and arbitrate privately, share wealth, tend to orphans and widows, exercise gifts, build the body of Christ, promote sexual purity, and settle lawsuits amongst believers. The civil

---

[27] Politics and civil government are not synonymous. The former deals with the pursuit of power and authority while the latter deals with its substance. Nevertheless, in this book I group the two together, sometimes using a form of politics and sometimes civil government.

[28] Genesis 1:26-30; 2:24; 9:1-3, 7; Deuteronomy 11:18-21; Proverbs 13:24; Ephesians 5:22-31; 6:1-4;

[29] Deuteronomy 14:28-29; Matthew 18:15-17; 28:19-20; Romans 12:4-8; 1 Corinthians 5; 6:1-5; Ephesians 4:11-13; James 1:27.

government[30] has the duties owed to God to promote good and punish evildoers. The civil government's duties owed to God of promoting good and punishing evildoers facilitate an environment where we may lead a peaceful and quiet life, godly and dignified in every way.[31] The civil government has no duty to *provide* good, nor can they compel general love.[32] That means that the civil government has no right to be the government doing the good; rather, they are supposed to protect and facilitate the individuals who comprise family government and church government, so that they are the ones who do *good*.

Governments render judgment and apply sanctions within each one's jurisdiction. The family government's sanctioning mechanism is informally known as "the rod."[33] The family government is to discipline children: "Do not withhold discipline from a child; if you strike him with a rod, he will not die. If you strike him with the rod, you will save his soul from Sheol"[34] The family government has no right to sanction those outside their jurisdiction.

The church government's sanctioning mechanism is informally known as "the keys."[35] The church government is to discipline believers and judge

---

[30] Genesis 9:6; Exodus 21:16-25; 22:1-15; Deuteronomy 1:13-18; 25:1-3; Numbers 5:1-4; Romans 13:3-4; 1 Peter 2:14.
[31] 1 Timothy 2:1-2.
[32] Exodus 35:4-5; 35:21-22; 35:29.
[33] Proverbs 23:13.
[34] Proverbs 23:13-14.
[35] Matthew 16:19.

insiders: "Are you not to judge those inside [the church]? God will judge those outside."[36] The church government has no right to sanction those outside their jurisdiction.

The civil government's sanctioning mechanism is informally known as "the sword."[37] The civil government is to promote good and punish evildoers: "But if you do wrong, be afraid, for he does not bear the sword in vain. For he is the servant of God, an avenger who carries out God's wrath on the wrongdoer."[38] The civil government's sword is physical and temporal, and it is to be used in those situations where one interfered with another's duties owed to God. The civil government has no right to sanction those outside their jurisdiction.

Nowhere in Scripture is man given the right to judge and sanction man's *intangible thought processes*. God has retained jurisdiction over man's thought processes. Only the invisible, transcendent anchor to reality knows our invisible thoughts and only the invisible, transcendent anchor to reality has jurisdiction over them. In Psalms 44:21 we are told that God "knows the secrets of the heart." In Jeremiah 17:10 God declares, "I the LORD search the heart and test the mind." And in Matthew 9:4 Jesus himself shows that he knows a person's thoughts.

---

[36] 1 Corinthians 5:12-13.
[37] Romans 13:4.
[38] Romans 13:4.

33

Do not be confused by how I use the word "government." A government is a God-ordained institution or structure by which rights are performed and facilitated. God is sovereign over the family, church, and civil governments, and for each government, He has assigned a temporal authority and jurisdiction. Here I simply point out that I never call the civil government "the government," for it is not. Otherwise calling the civil government "the government" asserts a humanistic structure where man (via the civil government) rules over the family government and church government. That is not the Christian paradigm. The Christian paradigm has Jesus as Lord ruling over not only the family government and church government, but also the civil government. So calling the civil government "civil government" (and not "the government") demotes man to his proper place, and simultaneously exalts Jesus to his proper place, above all.

Even though God assigned certain rights to the different governments, making them mutually exclusive, the family and church governments coalesce. When parents are fulfilling their teaching duties owed to God, as a function of that, if God so chooses, He will regenerate the child, causing him to believe what the parents have presented to him. The child is then adopted into God's church, and, thereafter, he or she has a new family.[39] Those children of God then know what the proper biblical paradigm is: the family government is the

---

[39] Matthew 12:50.

government responsible for education, specifically raising children in the nurture and admonition of the Lord; in concert those children that now comprise the church's congregation make sure the preacher continues to espouse how the parents have the duty owed to God to raise children in the nurture and admonition of the Lord, to the exclusion of the civil government, which is required not to interfere with but to facilitate that generational activity. The family and church complement one another and also hold one another accountable. That is the proper biblical generational paradigm.

As a precursor to what I elaborate on below, the Christian Establishment thinks that a humanistic society can be successfully engaged (and eventually overcome) by merely promoting how fathers are to teach their children the Christian worldview ... without getting political. Their theory rests in how the contemporary generation is lost, so the focus should be on the next generation. But that strategy fails due to a neglect to inform children that the civil government has no right to operate a school; as a direct result, the next generation of children is in the same predicament. That is, they are a generation who looks out into society and observes, *This generation is lost, so let us just focus on the next generation.* Their neglect to even merely teach their children (who eventually comprise society) about the civil government's lack of jurisdiction over the heart and mind is the very thing preventing a revival.

Governments, and their jurisdictions, are a zero sum. When one increases, another decreases. When the biblical truth that there are governments and that each has a jurisdiction are not taught to the next generation, then that next generation is left in a more difficult predicament due to increased civil government encroachment. Essentially, presenting the gospel to society can never be done successfully by abandoning how the civil government has no right to operate schools. As part of raising children in the nurture and admonition of the Lord, it must be taught that the civil government has a limited jurisdiction.

A failure to teach that civil government has a limited jurisdiction proves, over time, to be catastrophic to the gospel. To the detriment of God's Kingdom (to whatever degree man plays a role), when family government and church government fail to teach children how the civil government has limited jurisdiction, over successive generations, ground is lost. That is because, again, the governments are a zero sum; so when one's authority increases, another's authority decreases. So successive generations, as the civil government grows, having never been told the civil government has limited jurisdiction, allow the civil government to grow and grow. That makes the church government and family government lessen, suffering the gospel. The gospel suffers because humanists are then in the position to utilize their physical sword to advance their ideologies through civil government. Naturally those humanistic civil government actors are not facilitating the gospel, but hindering it. That this happens should be completely obvious to the Christian inasmuch as he supposedly believes there should be such a thing as limited civil government. He can only cling to limited civil government if he clings to how God limited the civil government's jurisdiction.

This, if it can be put in a nutshell, is the Christian Establishment's greatest folly; and whether done negligently or on purpose, the outcome is the same: when eliminating as part of the Christian worldview the generational teaching that the civil government has limits, future generations have greater difficulty advancing the gospel, since the civil government expands at the family and church government's expense. Remember, humanists—via the civil government's physical sword—are in the business of eliminating family government and church government—the spiritual sword. Here then is the war between humanism and Christianity played out in the public sphere. For preachers to ignore this reality—for preachers to purposely not get political—is to the gospel's detriment, as the humanistic civil government makes it more and more difficult for Christian truths to be propagated. In modern times the humanist is more faithful to his worldview than is the Christian; the humanist applies his ultimate authority to all areas of life, including civil law; the Christian does not, as the Christian Establishment says to teach children about Jesus' personal morality, but not His societal norms and *certainly* not His civil law.

When it is asserted we are to merely teach and preach personal morality to our children, to the exclusion of societal norms and civil law, it facilitates an easier contemporary humanistic civil government takeover. There is basically an abandonment of preserving society, as we are called to do (partly) via civil government. That is actually to the detriment of God's Kingdom, because future generations suffer due to increased humanistic civil government hostility to Christianity. The fact that the Christian Establishment should see this yet does not is grounds for their disregard and dismissal.

Within God's covenantal structures known as governments, there is the right to assert judgment in certain areas and, consequently, apply sanctions. Thus the God-ordained actors within each government have the right to judge and sanction, but only within their jurisdiction. Even though God is sovereign over all, He chooses to delegate to man; one area God has done this with is the promotion of good and the punishment of evil acts: civil government. God commands the civil government to be a sovereign. Not *the* sovereign but *a* sovereign. That is, He has given man the responsibility of representing God in enacting biblical law as civil law, and where there is a breach of that biblical law, man via the civil government is supposed to apply temporal sanctions. That covenant, and every other covenant communicated to man, requires its core content to be taught to successive generations, with the goal of communicating to subsequent generations about the institutions and structures that facilitate the larger Christian message that Jesus is Savior and Lord over all.

The fact that civil government is a God-ordained institution, required to enact biblical principles and then enforce them using force and coercion, is an essential Christian worldview component. *It is so essential to the Christian worldview that, without it, the Christian worldview cannot be passed down to subsequent generations.* A civil government that is comprised of humanists will implement and then enforce humanistic principles, all but eliminating the Christian's ability to advance the gospel. How the Christian Establishment does not understand this is one of the greatest lapses ever, and I am sad to say that it is so biblically obvious that the civil government must be Christian, that it is my assertion that the Christian Establishment's failure to know that can at best be considered negligence; at worst heresy.

ROMANS 13

If it was suggested that a family government or church government has the right to administer the death penalty (as does the civil government), society would rightfully protest. Or, if it was suggested that a family government or church government has the right to give a speeding ticket (as does the civil government), society would rightfully protest. Yet when the civil government does something outside their jurisdiction—like operate a school—society does not bat an eye. And the Christian Establishment runs for cover: Jesus was not about politics; let us not get political; let us not be divisive in arguing about whether to send a child to a civil government school.

Jesus was not about politics is a common refrain. The Christian Establishment perpetuates that Jesus did not come to get political. I actually agree with that assertion; Jesus' *primary* mission was about atonement. Nevertheless, Jesus did not come to start a temporal family either, yet we strive for that, to God's glory. That is, one could easily argue that Jesus did not come to do *this*, or Jesus did not come to do *that*. Jesus' mission was about atonement because only He could atone our sins. So it is true that everything besides atonement became peripheral, but that does not mean everything besides atonement became irrelevant. The late Dr. J. Vernon McGee stated in his Romans 13 commentary, "[C]hristianity never became a movement to improve [civil] government, help society, or clean up the town. The gospel was the power of God unto salvation of the individual."[40] Here, despite how I learned much from Dr. McGee, I drastically deviate from that perspective, on the grounds that after a man is justified, the gospel affects everything he does. Such a strong assertion that the gospel be compartmentalized to personal morality, and leave unaffected societal norms and

---

[40] J. Vernon McGee, *Thru the Bible: Matthew through Romans*, Vol. 4 (Nashville: Thomas Nelson, 1983), 736.

civil law, should be justified by something expressly stated in Scripture. Moreover, one would think that if we are to confine the gospel to personal morality and let it not permeate societal norms and civil law, Jesus would certainly have given us direction on how to be effectively double-minded, so as to be able to fulfill the task. Obviously, I disagree with McGee; whatever it is we do, even as a civil government actor, we are to do for God's glory.

The Christian Establishment thinks Jesus was not about politics, so they assert that *Christians are not supposed to get political.* We are not supposed to force Christianity on others, they say. This is not only an odd line of reasoning; it is inconsistent. That is because they are the ones who find it perfectly acceptable that there are civil government schools, which operate using the very thing they condemn: force and coercion.

So we are not supposed to get political? Would that not open the door to humanists then becoming the civil government, and then forcing humanism (and in some cases Christianity) on others? The Christian Establishment will never account for the inconsistency that Christians are not to force Christianity on others, yet it is acceptable for humanists to force humanism on others.

Sometimes a preacher does not want to get political, meaning he does not want to choose, for his congregation, between a Democrat or Republican.

But that is no longer an excuse, as neither party aspires to biblical public policy. If the preacher bothered to understand Romans 13, he would see that, and then be able to freely espouse how the civil government has limits, without the yoke of what they call politics.

Besides, at what point does it become acceptable for Christians to enter public policy? Is it when they comprise 51% of the electorate? Is it when they comprise 100%? If the latter, those Christians still need civil law, for they are still sinners. I assert the percentage is irrelevant; only one man is needed to espouse biblical policy. To say otherwise is to dismiss any prophet ever called by God to call His people into repentance.

Furthermore, what of the Establishment's claim that Christians cannot win back culture[41] via politics? If they are not teaching those of voting age that the Bible does not justify a civil government school, then how do they expect those people to ever be able to produce, through policy mechanisms, biblical policy, as even then only culture is targeted? Or, if they are not teaching those *not* of voting age that the Bible does not justify a civil government school, then how do they expect those young people to ever be able to produce, through policy mechanisms, biblical policy, as even then only culture is targeted?

---

[41] By culture I mean personal morality and societal norms.

A corollary to the refrain we are to be apolitical is that *Jesus did not come to establish a new political order*. Indeed, Jesus never expressly stated that He came to establish a new political order, although He did state that His Kingdom was not of the temporal world.[42] All that means, though, is that the Kingdom of God does not *originate* in the temporal realm. That is a recusal to those who think it is acceptable to evangelize through a civil government school: Christians are to invoke a spiritual source of power, one not of this temporal realm. In that regard, a civil government school's existence is not in accord with Scripture, as it relies on force to extract tax dollars, and coercion to compel a child's presence in the school. That is not reliance on the Holy Ghost.

Nevertheless, for argument's sake it could be said that Jesus (and Scripture as a whole) did not expressly address most things. To show how ridiculous it is to rely on silence to assert that Jesus did not come to get political or establish a new political order, it could be asserted that Jesus never came to enjoy a mint chocolate chip ice cream cone, participate in little league sports, or skydive. But that does not mean we cannot participate in those activities and do so for God's glory. Theoretically, anyone could refrain from a certain activity merely because Jesus did not expressly engage in it or address it. However, we are to glorify God in all we do,[43] and that, by default, presumably includes civil

---

[42] John 18:36.
[43] 1 Corinthians 10:31.

government. One would think something as powerful as the civil government, which is expressly commanded to use physical force, would need to be Christian.

Even if it is the case that Jesus did not come to get political or establish a new political order, does it then follow that there is not to be a civil government? In other words, if one claims that Jesus did not come to get political or establish a new political order, is it the case that there should *not* be a political order? If not, how do we account for Paul's words in Romans 13 and Peter's in 1 Peter 2:14? Or, if we are not to get political or establish a *new* political order, is the *old* political order still in place? If so, what is the *old* political order? And then how do we account for new nations developing over uninhabited land? What should their political order be? In answering those questions we are right back to where we started: discussing what civil government *should* be. Saying that Jesus did not come to get political or establish a new political order is not helpful, as the question still remains, *What is civil government supposed to do?*

If Jesus did not come to get political or establish a new political order, then the existing political order that was in place prior to Jesus is the model. But that still leaves unanswered, *What political order is that?* It could mean that the existing political order in place was from the Old Testament. Is that really what the Christian Establishment wants? Not likely. The Old Testament laws repulse them. If the

Christian Establishment preacher asserts that Jesus did not come to establish a new political order, then that means the old political order that was in place is to be the model. The burden, then, is on the Christian Establishment to answer what that political order should be. When the Christian Establishment espouses that Jesus did not come to get political or establish a new political order, then it is their obligation to articulate what civil government is supposed to do. It is not enough for them to say, as they are fond of doing, that they are against unrighteous civil government, but then at the same time leave unanswered what righteous civil government looks like. Merely saying Jesus did not come to get political or establish a new political order is at best unpersuasive; at worst it leaves those Christians who are involved with civil government with only an idea of what they are to work *against* and no idea as to what they are to work *for*.

Nevertheless, if the Christian Establishment cannot, with biblical verses, expressly show how Jesus did not come to get political or establish a new political order, then they are relying on theological constructs, drawing deductions or inferences from biblical texts that allegedly suggest that Jesus did not come to get political or establish a new political order. For example, in John 18, part of the biblical record of Jesus' arrest, Jesus said to Peter, "Put your sword into its sheath; shall I not drink the cup that the Father has given me?"[44]   But I think it is

---

[44] John 18:11.

incorrect to interpret Jesus' words to Peter as, "Do not be involved with civil government." Jesus was saying that only He was qualified to atone our sins.

A bigger obstacle the Christian Establishment has in asserting that Jesus did not come to get political or establish a new political order is that Jesus would then conflict with Romans 13 and 1 Peter 2. But both passages expressly address civil government and frame what civil government should be. That is, Paul expressly wrote, and Peter iterated, that the civil government is supposed to promote good and punish evildoers; so, essentially, the Christian Establishment says that Jesus' silence or theological constructs on political order are binding, yet Paul's and Peter's express statements about civil government are not. But are Paul's and Peter's words not divinely inspired, part of the canon, and, thus bearing on what civil government should be?

Does the civil government have limits? Yes, they do. In support of that, I do not present every part of Scripture to you. Books exist that more thoroughly address civil government. There is Gary DeMar's *God and Government* series, Greg L. Bahnsen's *Theonomy in Christian Ethics*, and Timothy Baldwin and Chuck Baldwin's *Romans 13: The True Meaning of Submission*. It is not that I am uninterested in presenting the hermeneutical nuts and exegetical bolts necessary to convince you that the civil government has limits. That proof exists persuasively. Rather, my goal here is to show you how God's Word does not justify a civil government school's existence; yet the Christian Establishment disengages that very issue, and, consequently, we incur God's curses that hinder the gospel. Most likely you have never been exposed to this information. To wit, the Christian Establishment.

The works cited just above properly espouse how the people have duties owed to God when it comes to civil government; but they also properly espouse how the civil government has duties owed to God. The Christian Establishment thinks we are to be subject to the civil government, but they do not think the civil government is to be subject to God. Bahnsen addressed the required double subjection:

> It is quite clear that Romans 13 has *two elements* in it: practical ethics and normative description. When both are not respected then the church ends up either with the distortion that the practical command to be subject means that normative authority is granted to anything the state might do (with minor qualifications), or with the distortion that the normative role of the state laid out by Paul must override the duty to be submissive

and grant the right of violent revolution.[45]

Bahnsen's point, set forth more fully in the context, is that what is expected of the Christian is also what is expected of the civil government: "After all, it would be initially peculiar if the Christian and the state were to be responsibly related to each other by Paul, but with the effect of laying duties upon the one while leaving the other to act merely as [they please]."[46]

My goal is not to hammer the Christian Establishment for saying we are to be subject to the civil government. I agree with them (and Bahnsen) on that, as Paul commands us to be subject to the civil magistrate. But the Christian Establishment's problem is they leave it at that. For various reasons they do not want to venture further. They, as I alluded to above, negligently omit how a magistrate's duty to God is to promote good and punish evildoers; they negligently omit how, if the magistrate fails in his duty, then he no longer fits the civil magistrate qualification. In that case we are not subject to him.

While Bahnsen's *Theonomy* is about how the Mosaic Law is binding as the starting point to every society's civil law, the thread permeating Bahnsen's line of reasoning is the same as that

---

[45] Bahnsen, *Theonomy in Christian Ethics*, (Nutley, NJ, 1977), 371
[46] Ibid., 372

permeating the line of reasoning set forth in Calvin's Institutes, which is that *both* the civil government and the people are subject to God. Calvin wrote, "We are subject to the men who rule over us, but subject only in the Lord."[47] I am not citing Bahnsen or Calvin as the ultimate authority, but both understood that Jesus is the Lord over all, and in that regard civil government is subject to the Lord. So, when Paul writes that we are subject to the civil government, it is not to be interpreted as putting citizens in absolute submission to those in the business of meting God's temporal sanctions.

It is within this part of Romans 13 that the Christian Establishment employs a distraction to shift the focus from being subject to the civil government, even unto the Lord, to the separate matter of God judging the nations. Their distraction is employed when someone points out how contemporary civil government is not promoting good and punishing evildoers, but rather promoting evil and punishing good doers.[48] The Establishment's response is, *God is judging us as a nation.* Calvin addresses how God utilizes civil government actors (good and evil) to judge others. Obviously, the historical record shows that was the case, many times over. Calvin wrote:

---

[47] John Calvin and Henry Beveridge, *Institutes of the Christian Religion,* (Grand Rapids, MI: Eerdmans, 1953), 988.

[48] Hebrews 5:14 requires us to distinguish between good and evil.

Herein is the goodness, power, and providence of God wondrously displayed. At one time he raises up manifest avengers from among his own servants, and gives them his command to punish accursed tyranny, and deliver his people from calamity when they are unjustly oppressed; at another time he employs, for this purpose, the fury of men who have other thoughts and other aims.[49]

But asserting that God is judging a nation requires hindsight as to whom God was judging. That is, when we look at the historical record, and the power struggles amongst the civil government and others, it is only with hindsight that we know what God's outcome was ordained to be. In other words, when dealing with supposed tyranny in the present, the issue of God judging the nations (dare I say) is irrelevant. That is because on an operational basis we do not know, within a current power struggle, who is actually being judged and what the outcome has been ordained to be. We just do not know, which is to say that the two matters of how we react to tyranny and how God is judging are actually two separate matters, as in the moment we are not privy to what God is doing with our lives, and what outcome He has ordained. The practical point is that, whether you admit to it or not, you keep

[49] Calvin and Beveridge, *Institutes of the Christian Religion*, (Grand Rapids, MI: Eerdmans, 1953), 987.

functioning in life, and you pray to God you are doing the right thing, even though you do not know in the moment what the outcome will be. To say otherwise is to assert, by illustration, that, when playing a basketball game against a most superior team, you abandon a good faith effort and quit playing after the first half because you think you know what the outcome will be. Yet no person knows what God's outcome will be. The Christian Establishment has quit.

A Christian's involvement against civil government tyranny could very well be God raising someone to punish tyranny."[50] All that is to say that, because no person knows in the present what God's outcome is going to be, it is necessary for each individual to exercise his duties owed to God. And that includes civil government actors, who do have limits and who are not outside the necessity of obedience to the ultimate authority.

When we look to Scripture it must be presumed that Jehovah, not man, is the ultimate authority. God never sets out to prove to humans that He is the ultimate authority. In contrast with empiricism, if God had set out to prove to man that He is the ultimate authority, that would have made man the ultimate authority; it would have made man the arbiter of what is true and false.

---

[50] The man could even be raised up peacefully, but still the Christian Establishment would condemn that as top down Christianity.

When one comes to Scripture—or for that matter, ignores Scripture—and participates in any semblance of reasoning, he or she must initially assume an ultimate authority. I illustrate this above relative to political reasoning. Suffice it to say then that God, being the ultimate authority, is an assumption—or presupposition—for which no convincing is required. It must be accepted on its face. If it is not, not only will there be eight billion ultimate authorities roaming the earth, but since there is no transcendent anchor to reality there are no such things as liberty, logic, uniformity of nature, meaning, mathematics, justice, sports, or superheroes. Nor must there be civil government, for if a Romans 13 reading is not preceded by the assumption that God is the ultimate authority, then there literally is no binding requirement for any civil government at all. *That reasoning applies to the Christian Establishment just as much as it applies to the humanist in search of implementing his version of salvation via the physical sword.*

God is the ultimate authority. "The heavens declare the glory of God, and the sky above proclaims his handiwork."[51] "The heavens declare his righteousness, for God himself is judge! Selah."[52] While God is the ultimate authority, he has vested ultimate authority in His Son Jesus. In John 1 we are told that everything was made through Jesus.[53]

---

[51] Psalms 19:1.
[52] Psalms 50:6.
[53] John 1:3.

In conjunction we are told in Ephesians 1:22-23 that to Jesus was put, in this age, "all things under his feet and gave him as head over all things to the church, which is his body, the fullness of him who fills all in all." Furthermore, we are told in Isaiah 9:6 about Jesus, that "the government shall be upon his shoulder, and his name shall be called Wonderful Counselor, Mighty God, Everlasting Father, Prince of Peace." God is the ultimate authority and He has vested that authority in Jesus, *the* government *over* civil government.

Some say that the physical, temporal realm in which we live is not something in which we are to participate. Consequently, they say, we are not to be preoccupied with civil government, because it is part of the physical, temporal realm. The suggestion is that one is considered more sanctified when he forfeits his engagement with the physical realm in exchange for the spiritual realm.

Rest assured, God's communications to us in Scripture, including how there is a temporal realm and a spiritual realm, are not meant to be out of touch with and inapplicable to the Creation in which we live. Church leaders oftentimes get so deep in the forest they can no longer see the trees; they get so deep with theology it becomes inapplicable to this world. Yes, God is the ultimate authority and He has vested Jesus with all authority. But those truths need not be so deep as to render them inapplicable to temporal life; it matters that Jesus is vested with all authority because it tells us the civil government duties, even temporal, are owed to Jesus. Most of our duties owed to God are temporary, including those relating to marriage and parenting. That does not make them inapplicable. The simple fact is that the civil government, in obedience to Jesus as the ultimate authority, is to facilitate the gospel, not impede it.

You need not take my word for it, for you can investigate this independently, but it is the case that God's people, over thousands of years, have been wrong about certain biblical concepts. (Martin Luther asserts antiquity is not dispositive of truth.)[54] Indeed, the Pharisees were wrong about who Jesus is; Roman Catholicism is wrong (amongst other things) about *Sola Scriptura*; 1980s evangelicals were wrong about how to affect public policy. To ignore the reality that God's people throughout history have been wrong is to ignore how *everyone* needs sanctification, and the possibility that the Christian Establishment is in error about the civil government operating schools.

If it were not the case that church leaders, looking back in antiquity, were never wrong, then what good was Gutenberg's printing press or Martin Luther's 95 Theses? Man is lost and still has the innate ability to misunderstand. The Christian Establishment is fallible and sometimes they too misunderstand: they have misunderstood Romans 13 and led the church astray on how the only way

---

[54] Martin Luther, J I. Packer, and O R. Johnston. *The Bondage of the Will*, (Grand Rapids: Baker Academic, 1957), 109.

that God's principles, stated through Paul in Romans 13, can be fulfilled is with Christians acting as the civil magistrate.

When we look at Paul's letter to the Romans, the theme is set forth in 1:17: "For in it the righteousness of God is revealed from faith for faith, as it is written, 'The righteous shall live by faith.'" In Romans we read the gospel presentation for both Jews and Gentiles, the doctrine of justification by faith. Thus, when we come to Romans 13, where Paul discusses civil government, we must not think that passage was arbitrarily inserted.

Romans 13 is a divide between God's sovereignty (written of in Chapter 9) and, within that, man's obligations to others, ultimately unto the Lord. Romans 13 bridges the practical theology before it in Romans 12 and the practical theology after it in Romans 13:8 to Romans 14. What comes before and after Romans 13 is Paul's admonition that we are to defer to God on matters of justice, and he divides his justice between temporal and spiritual. That is why Romans 13 transitions into being subject to the civil government, as we are then deferring to God. So what Romans 13 means to you, if you are not part of the civil government, is you (outside civil government) are to be about the gospel. Thus, Romans 13, within its immediate context, is not about civil government; rather, *it is about the gospel*. It is about the gospel because

Romans is about the gospel. Everything in life, including eating and drinking, is about the gospel, which means that when we come to Romans 13 and try to understand what Paul means, we must remember … *the gospel*. In that regard, does it make sense for Paul's letter to be so gospel emphatic, but then at Romans 13 Paul's gospel emphasis comes to an arbitrary halt? Or, in that same vein, does it make sense for Paul's letter to be so gospel emphatic, but then at Romans 13, Paul instructs us to be subject to a civil government that promotes evil and punishes good doers, in effect hindering the very thing we are supposed to facilitate – which is *the gospel*?

Because Romans is about the gospel, Romans 13 is about the gospel. Because Romans 13 is about the gospel, civil government is about the gospel. Because civil government is about the gospel, civil government is not to use the physical sword to advance the gospel, but to punish those who impede others who perpetuate the gospel with the spiritual sword.[55] This is one such way of articulating how the civil government is not to operate schools. Ironically, the Christian Establishment, who claims to be all in on the gospel, takes the position that civil government can do whatever they please, even impede the gospel.

When we look at Romans 13 it must be with the assumption that man is *not* the ultimate authority. In conjunction, we must understand that, because man comprises the civil government, the conclusion

---

[55] Paradoxically, then, it is still about the gospel.

necessarily follows that the civil government is not the ultimate authority.[56] Thus they have limits. More concretely, when the civil government is not in accord with Romans 13, the family government and church government have to work harder to be in accord with submitting to the civil government, due to approaching tyranny. But when the civil government is in accord with Romans 13, the family government and church government can do exactly what they are supposed to do, which is advance the gospel. That is not abstract theology; it is practical theology.

It is obvious we are to obey the civil government, for Romans 13:1 informs us: "Let every person be subject to the governing authorities. For there is no authority except from God, and those that exist have been instituted by God." While it is clear we are to obey the civil government, verse one should not be interpreted as giving whoever declares himself the civil government to be absolutely obeyed. That is because verse one does not tell us *who* is to be considered the civil government, a mechanism that is supposed to promote good and punish evildoers, which is so stated in verses 2-3: "Therefore whoever resists the authorities resists what God has appointed, and those who resist will incur judgment. For rulers are not a terror to good conduct, but to bad. Would you have no fear of the one who is in authority? Then do what is good, and you will receive his approval [.]" Verses 2-3 qualify *who* the civil government is, meaning, we know

---

[56] This is the Romans 13 Winning Syllogism.

who the civil government is, as they are in the business of promoting good and punishing evildoers. Verses two and three clearly identify how to legitimize a civil government: the one who terrorizes those who do evil. But the Christian Establishment will go so far as to assert that the civil government is without limits, so theoretically a person could qualify as the civil magistrate even if he is in the business of terrorizing those who do good and commending those who do evil. Yet again, even though there are topics we do not yet fully understand, should it at least be the case that the civil government is not to be considered legitimate when they are promoting evil and punishing good doers?[57] Why can't the Christian Establishment go so far as to adopt at least that Isaiah 5:20 principle?[58]

In Acts 5 "the apostles" were arrested and put in "public prison." Later Peter, despite persecution, asserted, "We must obey God rather than men." While I do not contend it is always clear what God's Law is in every situation—especially in contemporary times, in which we grapple with things like space travel and cloning—I do contend that where there is conflict between man's law and God's Law, it is God's Law that prevails. My latter

---

[57] Isaiah 5:20 Woe to those who call evil good and good evil [.]

[58] Isaiah 5:20 Woe to those who call evil good and good evil, who put darkness for light and light for darkness, who put bitter for sweet and sweet for bitter!

perspective goes against the Christian Establishment's theology, which is that the civil government is without limits, even in situations where it is unclear what God's Providence will ultimately yield. It is my contention that a more accurate Romans 13 understanding, in that we are to obey the civil government, is qualified to such a degree as to conform to that which is in Romans 13:2-3; otherwise, there yields the amazingly absurd result that the angel of the Lord, who released the apostles from prison, sinned against God, as he failed to obey the civil government. Or that Harriet Tubman (who covertly saved slaves through the Underground Railroad system) sinned against God when she disobeyed the civil authorities. Only an elitist theologian, or the Christian Establishment, would assert such things, leading American Christendom astray.

A helpful extrapolation is made in highlighting how in the United States it is a common practice to debate, criticize, and discuss the civil government. There are, in fact, within our civil government system, amongst others,[59] local, state, and federal civil governments. Amongst those civil governments, there arise conflicts about what the law is supposed to be. Legal conflicts are common, as there are fifty state civil government sets of law. Yet, is it the Christian Establishment's contention that it is unbiblical to move to another state if there

---

[59] There are parishes, counties, towns, cities, regional authorities, overlapping governments (like water districts), international authorities, and so on.

arises a disagreement about that state's law? I ask that question because it is equivalent to condemning a family leaving Germany[60] for the sake of being able to legally homeschool. If it is a sin to disobey Germany's civil government for the favor of the United States, then is it not the case that movement amongst states, for more favorable law, is also a sin?

Jesus is Lord over the civil government, and, therefore, the civil government is not the ultimate authority; consequently, man as the civil government is subject to Jesus. So not only does Romans 13:2-3 qualify how the civil government is supposed to promote good and punish evildoers, Romans 13:1, as other biblical verses show, comes with the import that whenever man is commanded to submit to another man, it is actually submission to the Lord Himself. To wit, look again at Romans 13:1. *Hupotasso* (hupotassō) is a Greek word that means to subordinate, to obey.[61] That same Greek word, designated as G5293, is used in Ephesians 5:22, commanding wives to submit to husbands "as unto the Lord." Do you see? Paul commands wives to submit to husbands ... as unto the Lord. That is, husbands do not have ultimate authority over wives; husbands are to submit to the Lord just as wives are to submit to husbands as unto the Lord.

---

[60] Homeschooling is illegal in Germany.
[61] James Strong, *The New Strong's Concise Concordance of the Bible*, (Nashville: Thomas Nelson, 1985).

Many other verses confirm that just because a human is commanded to submit to another human, it does not mean the latter is absolute. First Corinthians 16:15-16 commands us *hupotasso* those who have devoted themselves to the service of the saints, and *hupotasso* every fellow worker and laborers; First Peter 5:5 commands the young *hupotasso* the elders; First Peter 2:18 commands servants *hupotasso* masters; and in Luke 2:51, via Jesus' example to His earthly parents, children are commanded *hupotasso* parents.

Each *hupotasso* verse shows that humans have relationships that involve submission. There are even relationships we could surmise require *hupotasso*, yet they are not articulated in Scripture, like an employee *hupotasso* employer. Yet through these relationships, there is no assertion that the person who is to be submitted to is absolute, and in whom is vested ultimate authority. Otherwise, in the employee to employer scenario, would it not be a sin for the employee to quit working for a tyrannical employer?

Other verses buttress the contention that Romans 13:1 does not require absolute submission – not just because of the Romans 13:2-3 qualifications, but also how *hupotasso* brings with it the Revelation that Jesus is the authority (Lord) to whom we are submitting. Ephesians 5:21 commands each of us *hupotasso* another ... "out of reverence for Christ." James 4:7 commands us *hupotasso* God. And Romans 10:3 condemns those who do not *hupotasso* God's righteousness. In all those verses, we are commanded to submit to God. *But how can we be in simultaneous submission to evil man and a righteous God?* We cannot be, and that is why the Christian Establishment's assertion that the civil government is absolute is biblically incorrect.

Whether you are acting via the family government, church government, or civil government role, your title is not dispositive of your authority. Bahnsen wrote:

> It is especially important that one observe the logic of value-laden substantives when it comes to the description of someone as God's "minister." This is an honorific description of the person as ministering to God or for God. However, the fact that someone comes into the recognized station (or even office) of a "minister" does not guarantee that the evaluation "minister" is appropriate. For instance, from the fact that gospel "ministers" are described as not handling the word of God deceitfully (2 Cor. 4:1-2), we are not to be so foolish as to think that every ordained "minister" in a "Christian church" anywhere is above deceit in his use of Scripture. Not everyone

who claims to be a "minister" really is! In the same way, not every man who seizes power in a nation will *ipso facto* "minister" for God there. There are criteria that are expected to be, or have been, satisfied when a value-laden substantive is applied to a man. In this case a national ruler might be called a "minister" as a matter of course, but he would not actually be such a minister unless he matched up to particular criteria. Just as Paul can think of a "gospel which is no gospel" (Gal. 1:6-7), he certainly can think of a "minister which is no minister."[62]

So, incorporating the verses above, and how there is at least the implied but oftentimes express instruction that when being subject to another it is actually as unto the Lord, there are then limitations imposed on the human to whom we are commanded to be subject. While each person to whom we are to be subject has limits, there is no assertion that the limits are easily determined to have been breached. But that is why in Romans 13:5 we are told, "Therefore one must be in subjection, not only to avoid God's wrath but also for the sake of conscience." That means, for the sake of conscience, we are to be subject to the civil magistrate—as much as possible. Where possible,

---

[62] Bahnsen, *Theonomy in Christian Ethics* (Nutley, NJ, 1977), 369.

the benefit of the doubt is to be given to the magistrate. Nevertheless, giving the benefit of the doubt to the civil magistrate is a far cry from the magistrate having unbridled authority. Romans 13:5 is part of the larger context that obedience to the civil government assumes they are within their jurisdiction of promoting good and punishing evildoers; and where they are not and you act against them, you better be sure. When you are sure you have a clear conscience.

Romans 13 clarifies for what we are to pay taxes. In Romans 13:6 we are told: "For because of this you also pay taxes, for the authorities are ministers of God, attending to this very thing." The word "this" exists twice in verse six, and references verses three, four, and five, where there is mention and then iteration of the civil government's jurisdiction: to promote good and punish evildoers. *This* is why we are to pay taxes.

The Christian Establishment preacher will never condemn civil government taxes that fund anything beyond the administration of temporal justice. *Never*. And I can only speculate as to the reason that is so: the civil government is behemoth, and to limit their taxing power to merely supporting the administration of justice would offend a large percentage of the congregation, potentially affecting the preacher's paycheck.

Romans 13:7 is a continuation of verse six, relative to taxation, in that we are commanded: "Pay to all what is owed to them: taxes to whom taxes are owed, revenue to whom revenue is owed, respect to whom respect is owed, honor to whom honor is owed." Preachers, I am unsure as to how, seem to derive from verses six and seven that the civil government has unlimited taxing power. Somehow they miss the logical conclusion that taxes are not owed merely because a tax is levied, but because it is levied *and* also owed, as verse seven plainly indicates. That is, just because the civil government levies a tax does not mean that tax is proper. Note that I am not indicating that it is acceptable to not pay taxes, for that would be in the short-term (for most people) a serious detriment to the machinations of everyday life. However, that danger does not preclude preachers from articulating that verses six and seven plainly indicate that the civil government has jurisdiction over only promoting good and punishing evildoers, and it is for "this" that they have biblical authority to levy a tax. Anything beyond that is improper.

Upon my insistence that Social Security, Medicare, Medicaid, Obamacare, and civil government schools rely on unbiblical taxation, the Christian Establishment tends to respond that those are the symptoms and not the disease. In other words, they identify that pursuing public policy to undo improper taxation is the wrong way to go about solving the problem of civil government expansion. They are then, in that regard, not only impeaching themselves (as they admit they should be, but are not, addressing those "diseases" from the pulpit), but also properly identifying how culture produces policy. But that is the very reason why I am calling them out on not even *espousing* **(from the pulpit)** how socialism[63] is improper, so that people can first learn that is the case, and then go out into society and externalize that fact. But the Christian Establishment refuses to do even that. To emphasize the point, here is how that conversation plays out with the Christian Establishment preacher:

Kevin: Pastor, Social Security taxes interfere with my ability to tend to widows, orphans, and the elderly.

Pastor: That may be so, but those taxes are the symptoms [public policy], not the disease [disobedience to Romans 13 taxing limits].

Kevin: I agree, so why do you not address disobedience to Romans 13 taxing limits from the pulpit, so that congregants know that the civil government has limits, and then those congregants can teach that to their children, who will ultimately grow up and externalize proper Romans 13 public policy?

Pastor: Uh…

---

[63] Socialism means using the force of law (civil government) to take money from some people and give it to others.

Romans 13 may be *the* most negligently addressed Scriptures. There is very little to be confused about though, if one comes to Romans 13 just as he does its context, and that is with a presupposition that God is the ultimate authority and Jesus as Lord is currently in charge of civil government. In all of the Romans 13 discussion and analysis (or lack thereof), there is so much that requires correction. The Christian Establishment's lax disobedience and intellectual laziness accumulated over the last two hundred years has put us in a major contemporary bind. Whether the Establishment will humble themselves is between them and God.

Romans 13 is the heart of the civil government's jurisdiction. The civil government is to set the stage for the family government, church government, and others acting outside those two governments, to fulfill their duties owed to God. That is, the civil government is to *facilitate* duties owed to God, not *interfere* with them. And that is most certainly the case with taxation: when the civil government taxes for something (like Social Security) over which they have no jurisdiction, it interferes with the family and church government ability to gather and disperse funds privately with no gatekeeper fee.

The civil government is not supposed to exceed their jurisdiction, which means their duties owed to God are simply to promote good and punish evildoers. The civil government is not supposed to be the good doer, but rather get out of the way so others can be the good doer. The civil government, on all levels, must not exceed their jurisdiction of promoting good and punishing evildoers. Where they do exceed their jurisdiction it is not consciously binding.

One question posed above is, *Does the civil government have limits?* That answer is a function of the civil government's delegated jurisdiction, extending over only *actions*. By logical extension, then, there is no civil government right to use force and coercion to affect man's thought processes. As a result, they have no right to operate schools. That is the civil government's negative prohibition. As the civil government's jurisdiction extends over only promoting good and punishing evildoers, they have jurisdiction over only external actions, not internal thoughts. Attorneys are very familiar with this distinction in the criminal law context. *Mens rea* is a Latin term that means "guilty mind" and *actus reus* is another Latin term that means "guilty deed." Thus, in criminal law there are two inquiries: whether there was a guilty mind and whether there was a guilty deed.[64]

The fact that a criminal court probes whether someone had a guilty mind, or had *intent* to commit the guilty deed, is not justification for the civil government having jurisdiction over the heart and mind. That is because, when it is inquired into as to whether someone had intent to commit the guilty act, it is still the external actions that are judged.

---

[64] Strict liability laws do not have a *mens rea* component.

This is a completely biblical endeavor. Thus, in American law, the civil government must prove both the *actus reus* component and the *mens rea* component. The civil government must prove that there was a voluntary act accompanied by a guilty mind.

The Bible informs us about such a situation though, where someone causes harm to another but because there was not a guilty mind to do the harm to another, the person is not considered to have necessarily committed the crime. Deuteronomy 19:4-6 informs us:

> If anyone kills his neighbor unintentionally without having hated him in the past—as when someone goes into the forest with his neighbor to cut wood, and his hand swings the axe to cut down a tree, and the head slips from the handle and strikes his neighbor so that he dies—he may flee to one of these cities and live, lest the avenger of blood in hot anger pursue the manslayer and overtake him, because the way is long, and strike him fatally, though the man did not deserve to die, since he had not hated his neighbor in the past.

So a man was cutting down a tree and the axe head came off, killing his neighbor. But there was no evidence this was done intentionally, and so it was not considered intentional murder. Whatever you think the penalty should be for intentional murder, this situation is not worthy of it.

Understand that when the civil government judges intent, they are not judging the mind; they are, in fact, still judging external actions. Note that Deuteronomy 19:6 indicates that part of the evidence determining the killing was unintentional was that the man had not hated his neighbor in the past. And hate, like love, is judged by external actions.[65] This is not to say that the ultimate source that causes love to be externalized does not come from the Holy Spirit; it does. But we cannot *see* the Holy Spirit, only His effects.[66] Nevertheless, even if one concedes there is a judging of the mind relative to criminal intent, there is a night and day difference between that relative to criminal law, and what is done in civil government schools. The former is commanded, biblical, retrospective punishment; the latter is prohibited, unbiblical, prospective discipleship.

The civil government is supposed to judge actions. Romans 13:4 informs us that the civil government has jurisdiction over the evil *doer*, not the evil *thinker*. This, by the way, is the rationale undergirding the impropriety of hate crimes, which are crimes that carry an additional penalty because

---

[65] The book of James attaches significance to one's external actions as evidence that a person is regenerated.
[66] In John 3:8 Jesus analogizes the wind with the Holy Spirit.

of certain victim characteristics or beliefs. The civil government has no right to judge a person's heart and mind in that way.

God has retained jurisdiction over man's thoughts. Only the invisible, transcendent anchor to reality knows our invisible thoughts. Only the invisible transcendent anchor to reality has jurisdiction over them, and only the invisible transcendent anchor to reality can punish us accordingly. In Matthew 5:27-28: "You have heard that it was said, 'You shall not commit adultery.' But I say to you that everyone who looks at a woman with lustful intent has already committed adultery with her in his heart." Those verses reveal that certain thoughts are sin; only God can know those thoughts and punish them.

As it is the case that the civil government has no jurisdiction over the heart and mind, it is the case that the civil government has no right to operate a school. The civil government is commanded to deal with punishment, not discipleship. *Punishment* is the infliction of a penalty on a wrong doer, for the purpose of atonement, which, not incidentally, assumes there is a Being to which atonement is required. *Punish* comes from at least five Hebraic words and one Greek word. The overlapping concepts undergirding *punish* are: chastise, penalty, condemn, reckon, judgment, spoil, curtail, chastise.[67] The idea behind punishment, then, is to

---

[67] Rick Meyers, e-Sword, (Version 10.4.0. Accessed March 24, 2016.)

apply damages against the evil doer. Within the temporal realm, that is indeed the civil government's duty owed to God.

Punishment is contrasted with discipleship. Punishment looks backward; discipleship forward. The concepts undergirding *disciple* are: pupil, learner, teach, instruct.[68] The discipleship concept assumes a teacher and student relationship.

Regarding the civil government discipling our children, the late Roger Bern commented:

> Nowhere in Scripture is authority over men's minds given to Civil Government; and the coercive authority which it wields is incompatible with influencing men's beliefs by reason and conviction as contrasted with force and violence. Nor have those intent on exercising domination over others missed the point that the ability to dictate truth translates into the ability to control.[69]

The latter part of Bern's quote relates to how the current civil government is utilizing civil

---

[68] Ibid.

[69] Roger Bern, "A Biblical Model for Analysis of Issues of Law and Public Policy: With Illustrative Applications to Contracts, Antitrust, Remedies and Public Policy Issues." (*Regent University Law Review*, Fall, 1995), 175.

government to control us as Christians. They currently control American Christendom's heart and mind, and the Christian Establishment allows them to do so.

The heart and mind battle has played out before in the Commonwealth of Virginia. Quoting from Kerry L. Morgan's book, *Real Choice, Real Freedom*:

> Prior to 1786, Virginians lived with an established or official church. The Commonwealth also sanctioned an official "textbook" of common prayers. The people were compelled to attend the official church or else pay a fine. They were compelled to support its ministers financially. Their ministers were required to be licensed by the civil government. Taxes also went to construct and maintain church buildings. The people were compelled to attend a [civil] government-approved church and be exposed to the [civil] government's approved version of the Gospel and Protestant theology by a [civil] government-licensed minister. It made no difference whether the people agreed with those religious ideas or not.[70]

---

[70] Kerry L. Morgan, *Real Choice, Real Freedom in American Education: The Legal and Constitutional Case for Parental*

This prompted (future President) James Madison to argue against that paradigm. In June 1785 Madison wrote his *Memorial and Remonstrance Against Religious Assessments*:

> The Religion then of every man must be left to the conviction and conscience of every man; and it is the right of every man to exercise it as these may dictate. This right is in its nature an unalienable right. It is unalienable, because the opinions of men, depending only on the evidence contemplated by their own minds cannot follow the dictates of other men: It is unalienable also, because what is here a right towards men, is a duty towards the Creator.[71]

On January 16, 1786 the *Act for Establishing Religious Freedom* accomplished abolition. So prior to 1786 there was a civil government-established church with civil government-compelled tithing, civil government-compelled attendance, civil government-approved preachers, and civil government-approved doctrine. We have

Rights and against Governmental Control of American Education. Lanham: University Press of America, 1997), 97.

[71] James Madison, *A Memorial and Remonstrance, Presented to the General Assembly of the State of Virginia, at Their Session in 1785: In Consequence of a Bill Brought into That Assembly for the Establishment of Religion by Law.* (Reprinted at Worcester, Mass: By Isaiah Thomas, 1786).

the same scenario now, except "preachers" are "teachers." If an established church government repulses you, why does an established civil government school system not repulse you?

When civil government uses force and coercion to affect the heart and mind in a form described as a church or school, they are beyond their jurisdiction. The civil government then, in operating either an established church *or* school, becomes the evildoer by way of interfering with, instead of facilitating, duties owed to God.

The primary force and coercion mechanisms the civil government relies on to perpetuate their schools are (real) property taxes and compulsory education laws. Property taxes and compulsory education laws are similar in that they both assume the default is that man owns the subject of the law: property and children, respectively.

Regarding property taxes, the Christian Establishment reinforces how, by default, man (via some institution like the Internal Revenue Service) owns all property, and man (for palatable reasons called a "citizen"), as the possessor, stewards to that institution. But God owns it all, and man (a *citizen of Heaven*), as possessor, stewards to God. H.B. Clark dutifully wrote, "Under Scriptural law, all property—the whole earth—belongs to God, who is the only owner of property."[72] This is the framework for private property, a framework the humanists are constantly eroding while the Christian Establishment stands by in obedience to them.[73]

Today Christians take a backwards approach to taxation. That is, they look at how large the civil government is and wonder, *How would the civil government operate if we did not give them enough taxes?* But that is the wrong way to approach the matter. The first inquiry is about what the civil government should do: *What is the civil government's jurisdiction?* Only second should taxes be addressed. In foreshadowing the compulsory education issue, backwards reasoning is also oftentimes employed in wondering what entity would be large enough to educate children if there were no civil government schools. This is a logical fallacy (begging the question) in that when asking, *What (other) entity would possibly be large enough to educate our children if there were no civil government schools?* it assumes the thing to be proved; it assumes the civil government *should* be large, and, therefore, the civil government's largeness justifies the civil government operating schools. But the correct line of reasoning asks, *What*

---

[72] R.J. Rushdoony, "God and Taxes," *California Farmer* (16 Sept 1967: 88. Reverend R.J. Rushdoony positively cited Clark in his article "God and Taxes." In accord, Reverend Rushdoony cited Exod. 9:29; Deut. 10:14; Ps. 24:1; 1 Cor. 10:26, to show how the earth belongs to God.)
[73] This is the humanistic-pietistic alliance Gary North addresses.

is the civil government's jurisdiction, and, therefore, is there justification for operating schools? If that line of reasoning were employed, the civil government would be so small (based on their actual biblical jurisdiction) that in modern times people would gasp when prompted with whether the civil government could handle the burden and logistics of educating children. Besides, God will not be mocked. It is, in fact, the case that the family government is the entity large enough to educate children, for their teacher to student ratio is two to one, much more impressive than one to twenty!

The bottom line is that a perpetual property tax on a man's property amounts to *de facto* ownership. If the man does not pay the tax, the civil government physically takes the property. That is not a tax; it is dominion. *Humanistic dominion.*

Attorneys deal with what is called the *burden of proof.* There are many different burdens of proof and variances to them. But when dealing with a burden of proof, such as that used in a criminal trial (beyond a reasonable doubt), there is a default. In a criminal trial the default is that the defendant is innocent until proven guilty. It is the prosecution's burden to prove *beyond a reasonable doubt* that a crime was committed; otherwise they do not meet the burden of proof.

So when a child turns a certain age, as codified in a state's law, an education law applies. That state's law requires the child to attend school, but not just any school. By default, the statute requires the child attend a civil government school. How do I know that? The civil government, in some capacity, is the gatekeeper, and you must convince them that your child attends a "school." The burden of proof is on the parent to convince a group of civil government actors that a child is being educated according to a civil government-created statute. If the parent does not satisfy the civil government gatekeepers, the child must attend a civil government school. Do you see? By default, your child must attend a civil government school. The parent must affirmatively opt the child out of attending a civil government school. *The burden is on the parent*. That is backwards. This is why I say that your children belong to the civil government. *This should outrage Christians*.

The biblical paradigm holds that, by default, children belong to God. God has delegated the education duty to the family government, with the church government as the larger body God wants your child to belong to. God wants your child to be His, born again. The burden is on the civil government to prove someone committed an evil act; only then can the civil government step in, as they have the duty to promote good and punish evildoers. Unless the family government and church government are acting as an evildoer, the civil government has no role in the matter.

Both property taxes and compulsory education, which are the mechanisms that perpetuate each civil government school, are unbiblical. But while something emanating from the civil government is unbiblical, that does not necessarily justify disobedience. Indeed, Paul's words in Romans 13 frame the civil government's role relative to the gospel. Verse seven takes on a conciliatory tone in that we are to be amenable to the civil government, but yet again, for the sake of the gospel.

In *Romans 13: The True Meaning of Submission*, Timothy Baldwin and Chuck Baldwin write, "A genuine recognition of submission to a God-ordained [civil] government may require [civil] government reformation or resistance." A few sentences later they write:

> Paul asserts this dichotomy between obeying God's ordinance of laws made by ministers of God to thee for good and laws made by man for our mischief. Replacing bad [civil] government with good would be necessary to comport to God's command for submission to [civil] government in Romans chapter 13.[74]

Baldwin and Baldwin are helpful in their assessment that there is a resistance continuum with

---

[74] Chuck Baldwin and Timothy Baldwin, *Romans 13: The True Meaning of Submission* (Kalispell, MT: Liberty Defense League, 2011), 93.

reformation on one end and revolution on the other. If there were not, then one could argue that voting for a new candidate to office is just as sinful as revolution against the incumbent.

While I think involuntary slavery is worthy of armed resistance, the great Englishman William Wilberforce, God's human catalyst behind the abolition of the English slave trade, operated in the realm of reformation. Wilberforce consulted John Newton, a former slave and slave trader, on whether his regeneration better qualified him for church government over civil government:

> Indeed, the great point for our comfort in life is to have a well-grounded persuasion that we are where, all things considered, we ought to be. Then it is no great matter whether we are in public or in private life, in a city or a village, in a palace or a cottage. The promise, "My grace is sufficient for thee," is necessary to support us in the smoothest scenes, and is equally able to support us in the most difficult.[75]

John Newton, in his own words, did not think that regeneration disqualifies a civil minister for his office. It then seems to be a reasonable inference

---

[75] Kevin Belmonte, *William Wilberforce: A Hero for Humanity* (Grand Rapids: Zondervan, 2007), 137-38.

that Newton thought that praying for "kings and all who are in high positions"[76] did not necessitate that king or high position occupant resigning upon God's answer to prayer in regenerating the civil magistrate. Today's Christian Establishment seems to hold otherwise, and many would scold Wilberforce for his political involvement. The ideology behind Newton's advice to Wilberforce to stay involved with the civil government, and Wilberforce's reconciliation with that advice, acknowledged a law higher than man's, and that man's law should conform to that higher law. That is my point when I claim that whenever there is submission to another human it is indirectly always unto the Lord, the higher law. Thank God for John Newton and William Wilberforce.[77] The Christian Establishment would have told the slave, "Hang in there, Jesus is coming back soon," or "Hang in there, Christians are not supposed to be involved with changing society from the top down," or "We are not supposed to force Christianity on others."

Other humans have been humbled to the degree that they recognize Jesus, and not civil government, is the ultimate authority. Martin Luther King, whose commonly cited letter from Birmingham jail was an actual predicament, had no angelic relief, as did Peter. Yet there was still brave resistance. It is not my contention that when and how to disobey the civil magistrate is always clear; sometimes it is and

---

[76] 1 Timothy 2:2.

[77] I am aware that John Piper wrote a very short book about William Wilberforce. It leaves what I say later unaffected.

sometimes it is not. But it *is* my contention that the civil government has limits, and that they go beyond their limits when operating a school system.

Again, I do not pretend to have all the specifics of the application of biblical civil government principles. But the answer to misunderstanding is to work at understanding, not to throw one's hands in the air and take the easy way out, or falsely accuse those of us with a legitimate civil government calling of legalism or top-down politics. *Do some homework.* So the Christian Establishment preacher goes out on a limb and asserts we are all supposed to obey stop signs; that is not dealing with today's difficult issues. Such is the Christian Establishment, who makes little to no effort to understand. The Christian Establishment must better understand the Romans 13 arguments and tackle the tough questions.

When Christian Establishment preachers tell us that we are to be subject to the civil government, *no matter what*, it indicts other humbled humans, like America's Framers.[78] I hesitate not to censure humanism, past or present, but I am sure I would learn more should Patrick Henry or James Madison deliver a sermon rather than any Christian Establishment preacher. All that is to say that when preachers tell us that we are to be absolutely subject to the civil government they suggest that our nation was improperly founded. This has them adopting humanistic sentiment. Yet it was our Christian

---

[78] It also indicts Daniel.

Framers, with whom the preacher adamantly disagrees on obedience to civil government, who are responsible for the preacher even having the ability to stand behind the pulpit and declare antinomianism and pacifism.

As an attorney I have a special appreciation for people who come up with *bad facts*. *Bad facts* are those hypotheticals designed to suggest that a principle is improper. For example, *Does the civil government have the right to tax for, build, and then maintain roads?* (I say no.) But bad facts are a red herring, designed to distract from the principle or impeach the principle. But bad facts do not impeach a principle; rather, they demand that more specific principles be drawn from the general principles. The Christian Establishment, at least when it comes to civil government, does not want to sniff drawing specific principles from the general principles espoused in Romans 13 and other parts of Scripture. They would rather continue the myth that Romans 13:1 is the only principle worth paying attention to, and Romans 13:3-4 could not possibly be what determines who the civil government is and how they are limited. Guiding principles must come from Scripture with the common thread being gospel dissemination.

Christian Reconstructionists are Christians who apply Biblical law to all areas of life;[79] every Christian should be a Reconstructionist. But the people who write books about Christian Reconstruction, have (justifiably) as their chief complaint that their theological opponents do not bother to study Christian Reconstruction. If they did they would realize that all Christians ought to be Reconstructionists. In the highly informative work, *Christian Reconstruction: What It Is, What It Isn't*, Gary DeMar writes, "Most critics of Christian Reconstruction do not read carefully what we have written[.]"[80] I add to that what Augustine wrote about his pagan accusers: "Either they are too blind to see what is put before their face, or they are too perversely obstinate to admit what they see. The result is that we are forced very often to give an extended exposition of the obvious, as if we were not presenting it for people to look at, but for them to touch and handle with their eyes shut."[81]

In this work's Introduction I define the Christian Establishment as American Christendom's leaders,

---

[79] Gary DeMar and Gary North, *Christian Reconstruction: What It Is, What It Isn't*, (Tyler: Institute for Christian Economics, 1991), 82.

[80] DeMar and North, *Christian Reconstruction: What It Is, What It Isn't*, 3.

[81] Aurelius Augustinus, Gill Evans, and Henry Bettenson, *City of God* (London: Penguin, 2003), 48.

led mainly by Christian attorneys, preachers, and pro-family organizations, who refuse to address, debate, and discuss whether there should be a civil government school system. To iterate, the Christian Establishment does not espouse the fact that the Bible does not justify civil government schools, and that failure disengages the humanist civil government school system; a direct consequence of that disengagement is that fewer humans hear the gospel.

The Christian Establishment is just like other establishments. They are apparatchiks: the interconnected persons within the establishment ratify each other's ideas; they mock newcomers and those with whom they disagree; they act as gatekeepers to the Establishment's followers; they disallow new ideas to penetrate their audience.

An obvious establishment example is the Mainstream Media, that left-leaning, like-minded, and affiliated set of "journalists" who, on the individual level, decide what is news and how it is to be presented. They control what we see and hear; they control the facts.

The Christian Establishment does the same as the Mainstream Media: they gate keep ideas with which they disagree. In Bernard Goldberg's heroic book *Bias*, in which he exposes liberal media bias, he includes a letter from a gentleman who applauds Goldberg's bravery in exposing, from the inside, the Mainstream Media's bias. "All too often, the liberal media tend to load the dice in favor of their viewpoint, deriding as kooky or somewhat unworthy of serious discussion those positions they disagree with."[82] The Mainstream Media has a monopoly on news, even news through alternative media, like the worldwide web. This is not conspiratorial;[83] it is just acknowledging that people take a worldview with them wherever they go, even to work. So, through the Mainstream Media, stories are filtered based on what those establishment humans want others to be told. Each story is told the way it should be told, according to the establishment news deliverer. For those people who try to bust the establishment's monopoly or penetrate the way things are done, for the sake of the ideology and in the interest of furthering the establishment, the potential penetrator is kept out, marginalized, and neutralized. That is how establishments work. This is the case with the Mainstream Media, which rejects the Republican, conservative, and Christian; it is the case with the Republican Establishment, which rejects the conservative and Christian; it is the case with the Christian Establishment, which rejects the abolitionist.

Like all analogies, the one between the Mainstream Media and the Christian Establishment breaks

---

[82] Bernard Goldberg, *Bias: A CBS Insider Exposes How the Media Distort the News* (New York: Perennial, 2003), 236.
[83] Technically it *is* conspiratorial, as a *conspiracy* is when at least two people work together, even impliedly, to accomplish an end.

down. After all, the Mainstream Media has a different ultimate authority in man. But once again they are analogous: both the Mainstream Media and the Christian Establishment think Christians are losers.

The Republican Establishment is another establishment. Prevalent mostly in Washington, D.C., the Republican Establishment is comprised of those Republicans who are not complete conservatives. Oftentimes they are economic conservatives but social humanists, if that. They have very little desire to move the conversation to the right end of the political continuum, and they are content with large civil government, as long as they are in control.

The Republican Establishment, though, is not innocent and idle. They monopolize the power positions and gatekeeping mechanisms that filter the conservative message. They are the interns, the Senators and Representatives, their staffers, the media who buttress them all, and so on. This is not to say that they all are expressly conspiring together; but they, like the Mainstream Media, are like-minded, and so they reject other perspectives.

What I want you to understand is that there are groups of people who occupy power positions, who impliedly work together and who gate keep messages conveyed to the public at large; those groups are called *establishments*. The two major establishments are the Mainstream Media (who pushed conservatism into talk radio and internet communications) and the Republican Establishment (who caused the Tea Party groups to form).

Like in the Mainstream Media and the Republican Establishment, one establishment hallmark stands out: the establishment's people are self-contained. They all pay attention to the others in the establishment: they read each other's material, listen to each other's sound bites, and iterate the establishment's themes. Messages that conflict with the establishment have almost zero chance of penetrating that establishment's ideological network. Again, the only thing that can eliminate an establishment is the replacement of the persons who comprise the establishment and/or the mechanisms in which the people operate.

The brief elaboration on the Mainstream Media and the Republican Establishment is for preparing you to understand the Christian Establishment. The Christian Establishment is, of course, an establishment. Any idea that conflicts is ignored, marginalized, and if it gets to this, dismissed with non sequiturs and appealing to the establishment as a self-authenticating authority: *argumentum ad establishment*.

The Christian Establishment is comprised of American Christendom's leaders: preachers and ministers, their secretaries, bookstore owners, pro-family organizations, political organizations, university and seminary professors, teachers in general, radio station owners, and so on. They are the men and women who lead American Christendom and who own, operate, and control what messages do and do not get through to American Christendom. In short, they are in control. The Christian Establishment never debates whether there should be civil government schools. When that debate is brought to them it is quashed. They favor the status quo and do everything to protect that.

Here is evidence of that status quo:[84]

- Has your Christian *college professor* ever prompted you to think about whether it is biblically proper to use someone else's property taxes to evangelize?

- Has your *Sunday school teacher* ever prompted you about how, if you believe that the civil government has the right to operate a school, then you are a socialist?

- Has your favorite *pro-family organization* ever told you that Tim Tebow bills are unbiblical?

- Has your favorite *conservative media organization*, in condemning Net Neutrality, ever pointed out to you that we

---

[84] In the form of leading questions.

already have local boards gate keeping Christianity, in the form of school boards?

- Has your favorite *Obamacare opponent* ever understood that if the civil government has jurisdiction over a person's mind in civil government schools, then certainly the civil government has jurisdiction over a person's physical body?

- Has your favorite *political pundit* (Mike Huckabee, Michelle Malkin, David Barton, or Glenn Beck) ever questioned a civil government school's existence?

- Has your *youth minister* ever questioned compulsory education laws?

- Has your *local political group* ever declared, *Don't tread on me—or my child— in a civil government school?*

- Has your *local Christian bookstore* ever carried a book calling for civil government school abolition?

When necessary I am not afraid of calling out individuals and organizations that are in error; this whole book testifies to that. So, if any Christian organization does not believe civil government schools should not exist, then they have conceded every other battle in which they engage. I cannot stress that enough. *If the civil government may use force and coercion to affect thought, then it follows that they can use force and coercion to affect how we live.*

In one form or another, the Christian Establishment tends against many unbiblical behaviors in our society. They are against many things, except the very thing that produces the unbiblical behavior in our society: the civil government school system. By the Christian Establishment organizations dealing with (at best) singular problems, *to the exclusion of abolition*, they ignore the very thing causing the problems. To cite the obvious, they deal with the symptoms and not the disease. God's Word does not justify the civil government school's existence, yet the Christian Establishment disengages that very issue, and, consequently, we incur God's curses, which hinder the gospel.

Follow me as I deviate for just a moment to share with you how I came to understand all of this. When I was in law school, I had a conversation with a peer about starting a law school at a prominent Bible college in Chicago, the area where I am from. The respectful and frank response was that there is probably no potential there, due to that college's ideologies regarding how to advance the gospel. At the time I did not know what that meant; besides, I thought, *How is it possible for a Christian to be disengaged from law?*

Sometime shortly thereafter I participated in an Education Law Seminar in which private education was emphasized. As part of a project for that Education Law Seminar I visited a prominent home school legal defense association. I remember the visit like it was yesterday. In having lunch with one of their attorneys I was told, "It is okay for there to be public schools because there is nothing in the New Testament prohibiting them." I still remember looking at him not only in awe, but also disappointment.

At that time I was only beginning to put the puzzle together, wondering whether the Bible justified civil government schools. Looking back, it is hard to tell exactly when it was revealed to me that the civil government has no right to operate a school, but it was about that time. I was looking at culture and politics, I was looking at education, I was looking at the legal field, and I saw how we are doing everything wrong. We are not engaging the humanist's church, called the civil government school. Moreover (and this was the nail in the coffin), it was shown to me, through certain organizations, that Christians are arguing the wrong thing. They are stuck on debating (or more accurately, shutting down debate on) whether a child should be *sent* to a civil government school; they are not debating whether there should *be* civil government schools. The Christian Establishment is stuck on the delegation issue: *Should I delegate my education duty to the civil government?* They are not debating the jurisdiction issue: *Does the civil government have jurisdiction over the heart and mind?* This is *the* major mistake, as it completely bypasses the threshold issue of whether there should be civil government schools in the first place.

After I came to know that the civil government has no right to operate schools—and that Romans 13 (and complementary verses and passages) is a prohibition—I engaged people on this. That is how far I got. The Christian Establishment hates questioning the civil government's jurisdiction.[85]

In dozens of ways I engaged the Christian Establishment. I sent letters to home school convention organizers asking for booth space: rejection. I issued a public declaration that I would debate any Christian on whether the civil government has the right to operate a school: nothing. I spoke to my local church. I spoke with preachers at other churches. I asked Christian magazines to let me write about the issue: nothing. I called radio stations. I phoned, I wrote, I emailed: still nothing. The question as to whether the civil government has the right to operate a school bounces right off the Christian Establishment, almost like the gospel bounces off those with a seared conscience. I knocked; there was no answer.

Understand what the Christian Establishment is: preachers, Sunday school teachers, bookstore owners, legislators, professors, publishers, civil government school teachers, attorneys, pro-family organization leaders, convention organizers, and

---

[85] The modern church would crucify Oliver Cromwell.

church leaders—all Christian!—stuck in humanistic reasoning. They all affirm one another, as their infrastructure is interconnected and dependent on each other. And without a Supervening Cause, that humanistic reasoning will not be broken. Rush Limbaugh[86] correctly observes how conservatives cannot break through the humanistic Mainstream Media, so humanism is perpetuated. In that same way, the Republican Establishment operates. Still further in that same way, the Christian Establishment operates: The Christians currently in power positions affirm one another, and their circularity with the people (the congregants) will not be broken, *but by God.*

The Christian Establishment is the infrastructure developed over the last many decades. They ratify each other's books (without even reading them); they copy and paste the sermons before them; they are never exposed to Scripture but from one angle; they enter the pulpit without exploring other arguments. The Christian Establishment is insulated like a bunch of Ivy Leaguers; like the Mainstream Media; like the DC Establishment; like the Republican Establishment. They pat each other on the back and keep telling themselves to keep doing the same thing—but just work harder at it. They pat each other on the back whenever challenged, when someone like me comes along, who gets divisive, who questions the Establishment, who makes a good faith effort to disagree with what American

---

[86] Rush Limbaugh knows more about the Christian worldview than many preachers I know.

Christendom's leaders are espousing. They stonewall and ignore and give little attention to warn their flock that Jesus did not come to reign in a new political order.

The American preacher is the Christian Establishment's nucleus. The Christian Establishment preacher is out of touch with the real world, in what may be the biggest reason his station is analogous to that of other Establishments. Think about how different the Establishment preacher's Romans 13 sermon would be if he were to operate in the real world for a little while. Do you think that he would preach that Christians cannot be used by God in civil government if the preacher saw how civil government overtaxation disproportionately injures poor people, making it difficult for them to home school? Do you think his Romans 13 sermon would be different if he saw how the social security tax transfers the ability to care for one's parents to the civil government, or how that same tax injures small businesses? Do you think his Romans 13 sermon would be different if he could see how youth are punished by courts for not wanting to attend nihilistic schools? How much more applicable would a preacher's sermons be if he were a landlord, small business owner, logician, ditch digger, or attorney. He would apply God's Word as intended—as *directions* for how to do everything in life, not just *directions* to Heaven. "The duty of the theologian, however, is not to tickle the ear, but to confirm the conscience, by teaching what is true, certain, and *useful*."[87]

What if the preacher went to Iraq to see how the civil government there does not reflect biblical principles, tyrannizing a people who are not even able to openly discuss Christianity? How different would the preacher's sermon be if he saw how European businesses disregard God by polluting His Creation? The Christian Establishment preacher has no understanding how the butcher, the baker, and the public policy maker operate in the real world. What is more frustrating is he does not care; the Christian Establishment's Theology is akin to the Republican Establishment's theory: neither establishment understands the real world.

America is in a downward spiral, led by the Christian Establishment. It is my firm belief that God's Spirit is breaking that downward spiral. That is why, instead of causing me to join the Christian Establishment, God is working through me to demolish it. Through lawyering and a pro-family organization, I am doing my best to break the Christian Establishment's perpetuation of curses on America.

---

[87] Calvin and Beveridge, *Institutes of the Christian Religion* (Grand Rapids, Mich.: Eerdmans, 1953), 92-93. Emphasis added.

CHAPTER 3
THE CHRISTIAN ESTABLISHMENT DISENGAGES THE HUMANIST'S CHURCH

THE CIVIL GOVERNMENT SCHOOL SYSTEM IS THE HUMANIST'S CHURCH

I once told a preacher that a civil government school is a church. His response was that they do not fit the definition of *church*. Of course they do; they are a *false* church, one with a false salvation, a false conversion, a false worldview, a false eschatology, and so on. It is not God's body of believers; it is not *ecclesia*.

These are not overly philosophical topics, beyond your and my ability to understand. You and I have the ability (the command) to discern what a true body of believers is and what it is not. When you search for a church you are doing that very thing; that is, you are going into a physical building and inspecting the congregation's theology and their accompanying works. You are fulfilling God's command to discern truth from error.

Every Christian is in the business of inspecting what is a true church and what is a false one. Near where I live they built a new civil government high school. The school's name is Heritage (High School). When I drive by it I tell people, "Look, they just built a megachurch." *Heritage* is also the name of a church near me. That is relevant because you cannot always tell what something is by the name; you must look deeper.

Ask yourself, *What are the similarities between a civil government school and a church?* Some have the same name. Near me, besides Heritage, there is also a civil government school named Liberty and there is a Christ-centered school named Liberty. So the names do not always tell you whether the entity is a civil government school. Moreover, both entities have buildings made of the same materials; they have some of the same attendees; they have organizational structures; each teaches certain philosophies about ethics, the nature of reality, and how we know things. On and beneath the surface they have similarities.

Tangentially, the reason I call the civil government a "they" and not an "it" is because of how God's body of believers is a *people*, moving about in society. Your preacher has hopefully emphasized this very point, that the church is not a building but rather a people. So while the church government— the true ecclesia—is people, so too is any other government. Of course it is easy to assent to how the family government is a people and how the ecclesia is a people, but we must also think of the civil government as a people. That is not an irrelevancy, because it means that while the civil government should be led by Christians, the people that comprise the civil government can and do subscribe to falsities. The main falsity currently subscribed to is that the civil government may disciple our children. And that falsity is not empty: their discipleship contains false versions of salvation, conversion, worldview, and eschatology. So while I do think the civil government school system is an established church, I am not bent on you calling it one. Rather, I am bent on you knowing the civil government school system is *the* mechanism, church or not, for promoting humanism. Moreover, I am bent on you understanding that you are in the business of discerning the civil government school system's doctrines as true or false.

To have a justified, true belief that civil government schools are a false church is to have a sophisticated understanding of what a church is and what a church is not. It is to have a sophisticated understanding that sometimes things look similar, but they are in fact different. Yet, despite the need for sophistication, it is no more than what God prescribes us to have throughout the Bible. I have, in fact, encountered preachers who have very little understanding of how civil government schools are a counterfeit church; alternatively, I once encountered a preacher who, after discovering that I am an abolitionist, told me to my face that the civil government school system is a church! Some people understand a spiritual battle is occurring; one in which people, not buildings, are the participants.

There are two main differences between the church you send your child to for thirty hours a week and the one you send your child to for three hours on Sunday. First, one you finance involuntarily via taxes; the other you do not. And second, one your child attends involuntarily; the other he does not. When preachers hold that it is okay to send a child to a civil government school they are missing the point, which is that a civil government school relies on *involuntariness*. In contrast, God's church does not. So why is your preacher okay with Christian teachers "evangelizing" in civil government schools? Would a preacher be okay with the civil government compelling children to attend a Sunday sermon, and for the local community to be forced to pay for it to be delivered? They should not be, which is why they should not be okay with there being civil government schools.

The civil government school system is a church. Is there not a building, where people go to learn facts, which are a function of a set of principles that apply to the world around them? Are there not leaders and a flock? Are there not assertions about what should be societal norms and civil law? Are moralities not taught? Is there not an ultimate authority that anchors it all? To say that a civil government school is not a church is to ignore how a church—true or false—is merely a mechanism for advancing one's faith. The humanist uses the physical sword; the Christian the spiritual sword.[88] Call it whatever you want, nevertheless civil government schools are a counterfeit *ecclesia*.

---

[88] I do not subscribe to the two kingdoms theology.

Revisit Morgan's thesis, which is that disestablishing civil government schools is analogous to church disestablishment in late 1780's Virginia. That is, the established church had civil government-compelled tithing, civil government-approved doctrine, civil government-compelled attendance, and civil government-approved preachers. But now reconsider Morgan's thesis, this time with the (true) assumption that some Christians send their children to a civil government school and some do not. Is it proper for one side of the Sunday congregation to use force and coercion to take money from the other side of that same congregation, all under the banner of the supposed freedom to send a child to a civil government school? Of course not, so do not think for a moment this is about the supposed option of sending a child to a civil government school. It is not about that. It is absolutely about whether a Christian can use force and coercion to take money from other Christians. That is why education is not about delegation but jurisdiction.

I will challenge you further. Suppose you had two pictures in front of you, but the two pictures were exactly the same: two medium-sized brick buildings. You had no other information in the pictures. Then, suppose you were told, this building is a "church" and this is a "civil government school." Then you were prompted to explain why it is okay for someone to be compelled to attend this building but not the other building. What would be your response? The Christian Establishment has no response. They just ignore the issue. That is what makes them the Christian Establishment.

Between the two churches there are two different approaches to sin. I once told a preacher that the civil government school system is the disease, and the humanistic society we are currently antagonized by are the symptoms. He kindly responded that sin is the disease. Obviously, he is correct. But my (attempted) point to him was that the source, origination, and ground zero for our nation's societal decline is the humanist's church—the civil government school system. If sin is, in fact, the disease, civil government schools do nothing to bring the disease to their congregants' attention; they, in fact, do just the opposite, which is they disregard the very idea of sin, and that there is even an objective right and wrong. They do nothing to lead sinners to the cure, Jesus.

There is nothing hands-off in the humanist's church more true to their ultimate authority than the Christian. Excitingly, their church is not truncated and compartmentalized, but rather extended and comprehensive. Their god is (supposedly) huge and he affects every part of life. It is a fact that the Trinity has no equal; but from the Christian Establishment generally, and the Christian pulpit specifically, God is small.

THE CHRISTIAN ESTABLISHMENT DISENGAGES THE HUMANIST'S CHURCH

I participated in the Inaugural Great Education Forum in 2015 in Virginia. Five speakers each addressed differently the question, *Should the church use public schools?* Naturally, I rejected that question altogether and explained how there should not be civil government schools in the first place.

One speaker at the Forum, though, made the (private) assertion that winning back society was through mere Christian education, and that my abolition assertion was not only unnecessary, but not the way to win back society. Herein is the Christian Establishment's foolishness. On its face that plan has an obvious flaw in that it ignores how Christian education and abolition are two sides of the same coin.[89] The heavens rejoice when a child is withdrawn from a civil government school. But what remains is the civil government still possessing our money. So, the answer is not promoting private education, nor is it promoting abolition. The answer is both sides of the coin are needed. Decreasing civil government schools will occur by increasing Christian education; Christian education will increase by decreasing civil government schools.

The speaker's crack becomes a fissure upon further analysis. The Christian Establishment has failed,

---

[89] It is the same with abortion. Christians must be pro-life *and* anti-abortion.

over and over and over again, by *merely* teaching the next generation about Jesus. What could be wrong with that, you ask? How could it be insufficient to teach the next generation about Jesus? Teaching the next generation about Jesus is certainly something I do not condemn. But *merely* teaching the next generation about Jesus is insufficient; that is because that next generation is not being told about how there should not even be civil government schools.

You see, the Forum speaker's opinion was that teaching the next generation about Jesus was enough because eventually that next generation would grow up and then teach their children about Jesus. So in his mind, *Problem solved, we win back society by proclaiming Jesus to individuals, and when the numbers grow large enough, we have won back society.*

The problem with that thinking is that it never gets our jurisdiction back. In fact, the children who were taught merely about Jesus grow up to be just as ignorant about civil government as were their parents. That subsequent generation then does what? They look upon the landscape and see societal decline (with their own childhood as a benchmark) and then say to themselves, *The way to win back society is to teach our children (merely) about Jesus.* Do you see the problem with that thinking? It is a downward spiral that is attached to the falsity that both the Christian church and the humanist church can coexist. Over and against the

Christian, the humanist acknowledges the truth that the Christian church and the humanist church are a zero sum.

Understand that when I talk about how foolish it is to merely teach the next generation about Jesus, I am talking about how the next generation is merely told that Jesus is the Savior, and maybe taught to some small degree about how He is Lord, and that after regeneration those Christians are supposed to evangelize that Jesus is the Savior. Under that paradigm there is no generational teaching about externalizing Jesus within the civil government realm. Thus, subsequent generations never learn about civil government limits, and, naturally, they never do anything about the civil government exceeding their jurisdiction. Over the course of American history, there developed civil government schools, then Social Security, followed by socialized medicine and other socialistic programs. There was and still is constant civil government expansion. And because the family government, church government, and civil government are a zero sum, every time the civil government expands, the other governments contract. This is not theoretical: a civil government school steals jurisdiction from the family and church governments; a Social Security tax lessens the Christian's ability to tend to the elderly; socialized medicine obstructs the Christian's ability to tend to the poor. If the next generation is never taught that civil government schools are biblically improper, then the downward spiral is never stopped. Subsequent generations must be taught about the civil government, otherwise we are frogs sitting in a pot coming to a boil. This is not to say that every Christian is called to be a civil government minister, but the knowledge that the civil government has limits is used by everybody to at least check, through the ballot box and public discourse, those in civil government. *The biblical knowledge that the civil government has limited jurisdiction must be passed on to the next generation.*

A sophisticated understanding of what is happening in the United States requires you to understand what happens on the humanist side of things, relative to society. First, know that, on the humanist side, the problem is not ignorance of how the gospel penetrates all areas of life; the problem is gospel suppression. The humanist looks at society[90] and perceives a problem; in order to solve that problem, he acts through the civil government. So, in contrast with the Christian, the humanist does "evangelism" through the civil government and the physical sword; that is because his ideas must be advanced via force and coercion, otherwise they would never move forward. For a Christian to not teach his child how the humanist misuses civil government is no less than negligence.

---

[90] In some instances, especially this one, the term "culture" could replace "society." But I chose the latter because it seems to encompass all of life, whereas some consider culture to be society minus politics and civil government.

This idea about merely teaching Jesus to subsequent generations, with abstention from addressing civil government limits, falls on the Christian Establishment as a whole, but is concentrated on the Establishment preacher. He is the one with the most exposure to American Christendom, How else would Christians learn about civil government and then be able to put humanists on notice that they have limits? We all know the difference between coercion and love. God has made it plain to us. That matters because it is the Christian's duty to express through words and actions, towards the humanist, that he has limits. It is the preacher's duty to preach this. The fact that he fails to do so makes me wonder if he really thinks Revelation is our source of knowledge.

When humanists look out into the society, perceive a problem, and then pass laws to "fix" the problem, they, of course, make things worse. That is because humanists, by definition, are looking to man's ways to "fix" problems, to the exclusion of God's Word informing them about what should be done to solve a problem. For example, humanists look out into society and see how some people are hungry. So a law is passed using force and coercion to take money from some people and give it to central planners, who then first pay themselves a salary before feeding people who are hungry. Civil government central planning cannot work; *it is economically impossible* because God ordained it not to work. The problem, in fact, gets worse, because now more people are hungry. Curses have been brought down on us due to disobedience to God. The spiritual church (via the spiritual sword) is supposed to share belongings in order to feed and help one another; there is no gatekeeper fee.

But, of course, the fact that the humanist's policies trigger curses on society does not deter the humanist. He is, after all, suppressing the truth in unrighteousness. But the Christian Establishment does not tell them that the curses they cause on society are improper; after all, the pulpit says the solution to the problem is not political. (*No doubt* the solution is not political; the solution is to preach the gospel of Jesus Christ and that He is Savior and Lord over all, including civil government and politics. Saying so from the pulpit is not politics, it is the gospel and its out workings!) So what does the humanist do after he passes a law that is designed to "fix" the hunger problem? He sees that there is still a hunger problem; maybe he even sees that the problem has worsened. Yet he sees no correlation between his humanist policy and the problem, now worsened. So he passes another humanist law. In other words, he takes the same path to destruction over and over again; he is in a rut that he caused, and he continues on the same course over and over, further deepening the rut.[91]

Like the humanist via civil government, the Christian Establishment has American Christendom in a rut. The Christian Establishment

---

[91] Humanists at the top know exactly what they are doing in enacting policies antithetical to Christianity.

looks out into society and perceives that there is a problem. Then they declare, *It is getting pretty bad out there, so we better win back society*. Then, in order to win back society, they determine that the problem is not political but spiritual, so they say, *Let us work harder at teaching the next generation that Jesus is the Savior*. Yet they do not teach their children how to externalize Christianity and how to do everything with the driving assumption that Jesus' lordship extends over civil government. In that regard they never teach their children about civil government limits, because, after all, the solution is not political. Thus, the next generation grows up, and some of them (thank God) are regenerated. But the very rotten society they were supposed to engage and neutralize (by apparently merely growing older) never changes. In fact, it gets worse. It gets worse because the humanist civil government is never engaged and neutralized. It is gratuitous to say that the Christian Establishment is like a one-legged duck swimming in a circle. They have one leg promoting Jesus as the Savior, but the leg promoting *jurisdictional recovery* is nonexistent. The duck swims in a circle, never getting out of that circle, never getting out of that rut, never getting out of that cycle. The Christian Establishment needs a Supervening Cause to break that cycle.

I can compare what the Christian Establishment does to what humanists do because both groups disregard God, causing societal curses. They both think they are solving a problem, but the problem just gets worse. The humanist sees a problem and then convenes a committee, levies a tax, and enacts regulation. Well, the Christian Establishment sees a problem and then convenes a retreat, holds seminars, workshops, revivals; but none of it works, because they are merely in the business of promoting how Jesus is the Savior, and the jurisdiction issue is ignored. Thus the vacuum is filled by humanistic societal norms and civil law. Things get worse.

The Great Education Forum speaker I referenced above was so close, yet so far away from being correct in his assessment that we need to tell the next generation about Jesus. That is so true; we do need to tell the next generation about Jesus. But we also need to tell the next generation about how Jesus is the Savior and the Lord over everything—and that Jesus' lordship is over the civil government. Consequently, the civil government is not the ultimate authority and they have limits. Those limits preclude the civil government having jurisdiction over the heart and mind.

ROMANS 13 NEGLIGENCE

The Christian Establishment disengages the humanist's church, the civil government school system. One way this is done is through Romans 13 negligence. Negligence is the failure to do something that should be done, or in doing something failing to conform to a standard. I write *negligence* because I want to be fair; it leaves the door open for each individual to determine, between him and his God, whether his Romans 13 negligence is done purposely.

Oftentimes I hear the Christian Establishment attack the straw man that we cannot change society via politics. I see this attack most often direct towards Theonomists[92] and Tea Party members. You may be surprised to know that I agree that we cannot change society via civil government and politics; we cannot change society from the top down. Gary DeMar agrees, as do other Theonomists[93] and Tea Party members. But what the Christian Establishment is so used to rejecting is the notion that a Christian can be called to lead in civil government and politics. That is, the Christian Establishment sees someone involved, say, with the Tea Party, and they automatically think that the person is trying to change society from the top down. While there are always exceptions, the Tea Party is not trying to change society from the top down. In fact, based on my own experience with the Tea Party *and* Theonomists, they have keenly recognized that a major part of the American decline is due to the pulpit's disengagement. Many in the Tea Party are just doing what the preacher

---

[92] American Vision, "Not Imposing Christianity Through National Law," https://www.youtube.com/watch?v=FMZp_5GtAk8. (Checked on March 25, 2016.)

[93] A *Theonomist* would not think society can be changed via politics, since his perspective of law (mainly Mosaic Law) tends to be that the law was not designed to be salvific. I agree.

failed to do: declare to the civil government, "Woe to those who call evil good and good evil."[94]

The Christian Establishment's Romans 13 negligence crowd actually causes societal decline. That is because not only do they fail to recognize that Christians are called to be the civil government, but they fail to recognize that the civil government has limits. So, not only do they at least impliedly suggest Christians should not be the civil government actors, but that when humanists take our place as the civil government, per the Christian Establishment, they have no limits. Of course, in being the civil government, they are going to be more true to their doctrine and advance further and further into God's church, wanting to put us out of business.

The civil government is unique; so is the church government. What makes the latter unique is Jesus, and Jesus informs us about all areas of life. It is not man via the civil government that informs Jesus; it is Jesus that informs man via the civil government. However, the Christian Establishment preacher, with his "top down" critique, instead espouses a "bottom up" mentality. That sounds warm and fuzzy on the surface, until we realize that the preacher's bottom-up mentality can never produce a civil government that promotes good and punishes evildoers. *How do I know that?* Because once the regenerated "bottom" goes out and tries to be the "up," they have no idea what to do! *And why is that?*

---

[94] Isaiah 5:20.

Because the "bottom-up" preacher never articulated civil government limits, since he is against salvation by legislation! The proper generational paradigm is bottom up—*with* the truth that the civil government has limits.

It is true that we cannot change society via civil government and politics. Yet, despite the Christian Establishment's infatuation with that straw man, I know of no Christian who thinks otherwise. The mistake the Christian Establishment makes, though, is failing to teach our children that the civil government has limits. In iterating the above generational analysis, the current Christian Establishment looks out into society and sees how it is producing rotten fruit. Then they deduce, *We have lost this generation, so let us focus on the next generation.* But then, in focusing on the next generation, they fail to teach how the civil government has limits. Thus, the next generation grows up and does the same thing the preceding generation did: they fail to teach their children that the Bible limits the civil government. But over the generations, each sees a society that is even worse that than the one before; nevertheless, there is never a passing on to the next generation that the civil government has limits, so God's church gets smaller and smaller and civil government gets bigger and bigger.

To be blunt but accurate, the Romans 13 negligence crowd sticks it to their fellow Christians. A direct consequence of the failure to articulate civil government limits is that the part of the congregation privately educating is forced to pay money (taxes) to that part of the congregation that sends a child to a civil government school. And devastatingly, the Christian Establishment leaders quash debate on that very issue, confusing the jurisdiction issue with the delegation issue, and, thus, categorizing a jurisdiction debate as a disputable matter or preference. But debating the jurisdiction issue precludes the necessity of debating whether to delegate a child's education to the civil government. What I mean is, if the preacher properly espoused how the civil government has no jurisdiction over the heart and mind, there would be no need to debate anything that assumes otherwise. However, the Christian Establishment fails to hold there are limits to what humans acting as the civil government can do. In following that lead, American Christendom walks around as if there is no problem. Meanwhile, billions of dollars are forcefully taken by the civil government for the purpose of promoting humanism; but more specifically, billions of dollars are taken from one part of the congregation and given to another part. The preacher is not brave enough to articulate how the Bible does not justify a civil government school's existence, so he tells his congregation to not argue about delegation, getting him off the hook from having to articulate whether the civil government has the right to operate a school. This pleases the congregation's civil government stakeholders; it does not please God.

Imagine the scene, if you will, by stepping behind the pulpit for a moment. You are the Sunday preacher, and you have just told your congregation *not* to debate whether to delegate a child's education to the civil government. Thus, the congregants who do send a child to a civil government school are relying on the forcefully extracted tax dollars of those who do not. The latter congregants send money to the humanist civil government, who then receive a percentage "take," before sending the money to humanistic teachers, administrators, and other pharaohs. And all of that is supposed to be categorized as disputable and preferential.[95] The Christian Establishment preacher could stop all this; he does not. Instead, those in disagreement are shut down from even discussing the jurisdiction issue.

What is worse is that those who shut down attempts at even debating Romans 13 accuse people like me of legalism, attempting to impose personal preferences on others, being divisive, or clinging to *worldliness*,[96] as if people like me are not all in on God's spiritual Kingdom.

The legalism accusation is without merit, as there is no assertion that external conformity with a

---

[95] Why is it preachers get to decide what is disputable and preferential? Why is abortion not considered disputable and preferential, since there is no express New Testament prohibition?

[96] Apparently meaning someone who is focused on the temporal realm and not the spiritual realm.

principle causes internal regeneration. God causes internal regeneration via His Holy Ghost, not an external law. And the disputable matter or preference categorizing is irrelevant, since there is no assertion relating to delegation. In other words, it is a *non sequitur* to respond with disputable matter or preference, as it has nothing to do with how the civil government has no right to operate a school. The debate should be about whether the civil government has the right to operate a school. *The jurisdiction issue preempts the delegation issue.*

Like all the other charges against people who want to debate Romans 13, the divisiveness accusation too is without merit. First, if what qualifies as divisive is that which should not be discussed, then Jesus should not be discussed. Jesus is without a doubt the most divisive concept in the history of mankind. Moreover, to preclude debate and discussion about what qualifies as divisive hovers around humanistic philosophy; that is because it is the humanist who wants to settle issues at their lowest common denominator—to the exclusion of whatever is subjectively divisive or repugnant. That is supposed to be the very values clarification the Christian should be against. And it very well may be the reason so many congregations have such a superficial understanding and application of the gospel, as so many elements (like repentance and obedience) have been eliminated.

Even further, something categorized as divisive could just as arbitrarily be categorized as galvanizing, meaning arbitrarily labeling something divisive unnecessarily causes congregants to forbear a greater understanding and obedience to our Lord, no matter the outcome of the debate. Debate and discussion amongst Christians, if handled properly, produces sanctification for those truly willing to be obedient to Jesus. What else could a preacher want from a congregation than a more sanctified congregation—even one smaller than before? Does iron not sharpen iron? Indeed, it does not, if iron never confronts iron.

Second, the divisiveness accusation is really just appealing to the majority. When I was younger my mother would command me to do something and in response sometimes, instead of obeying, I would ask, *Why should I do that?* My mother would respond, *Because it is my house.* Then I would tell her that we should go outside to discuss the matter, because then she would need to invoke a different argument. While I discourage that type of disobedience, I can say that if there is a disagreement about whether there should be civil government schools, why is it that the people currently in the pews are right just because they were there first? When I challenge whether there should be civil government schools and the preacher unilaterally labels my assertion divisive, why is my assertion the divisive one? Why is it not the pastor's? Why is it not the congregants' who think there should be civil government schools?

Going outside the physical church, just like going outside the house, sheds more light on how absurd the divisiveness accusation is. Somehow the preacher deems the civil government school proponent to *not* be divisive, yet the opponent *is*? Why? What if I (and a hundred other civil government school opponents) was in the pew first, and then the civil government school proponents came along? Would it then be the case that *they* were the divisive ones? Moreover, would the preacher quell other issues as divisive, just because there is disagreement? What about the issue as to whether Jesus came in the flesh? What about whether there is a Trinity? What about whether a woman can be a pastor? Must we not debate those things merely because they are divisive?

Finally, and still regarding those who shut down attempts at even debating Romans 13, the "all in" accusation is without merit. That accusation is tantamount to saying that those who argue that the civil government has limits are clinging to this world and to the temporal realm. It is an amateurish accusation, as it is an uninformed, reflexive Christian Establishment response, who they themselves, by definition, have never engaged the threshold issue about whether there should even be civil government schools, so they cannot hold they are all in on God's spiritual realm.

For those who claim to be all in on Jesus, to accuse the abolitionist of not being all in is to really misunderstand what the latter group is pursuing in this temporal realm: obedience to Jesus within the legitimate, God-ordained civil government institution. Again, to say otherwise is to unnecessarily blunt one's pursuit of limiting the civil government to applying the physical sword to those areas of life that relate to temporal justice. In that regard, the argument is turned against the accuser: it is the civil government school proponent who thinks the civil government may use the physical sword to disciple our children. *He* then fails to be all in on God's spiritual Kingdom.

Instead of being all in, the civil government school proponent actually works against people like me and those who are merely trying to raise their children in a Christian environment. The Romans 13 negligence crowd adopts the humanist mechanism (known as force and coercion) and applies it in the education realm. Then they act as if they are doing God's Kingdom a favor by working for, and sending their children to, those civil government schools, allegedly bringing that same all-in mentality to a godless school environment. Then what they do is negligently shut down conversation on the matter, for unity's sake. The essence of it all is that the Christian Establishment works against Christians who think that Christianity (God's Holy Ghost) should be externalized in all areas, precluding the civil government school's existence.

Despite how you may disagree with me as to whether the civil government has jurisdiction over a child's heart and mind, there are still lingering issues relating to a student or employee entering a civil government school for evangelism purposes. In a civil government school, it is unlikely that the gospel can be presented the way it is commanded to be presented, facilitating repentance and regeneration. Granted, I concede that some have been regenerated in a civil government school. Nevertheless, civil government school evangelism is the gospel restrained; private Christian education is the gospel *un*restrained. Furthermore, it is debatable whether it is even necessary to evangelize in a civil government school. I can *almost* understand a Christian teacher in, say, Germany working in a civil government school, since home schooling is illegal there. But, in America, private education is perfectly legal (according to man's law, that is), and so is it really all in when the Christian would rather work for a civil government school, where Jesus is legally prohibited from being the rationale for all thought? Should the Christian even be teaching in a civil government school in light of how his salary is comprised of dollars obtained via force and coercion, and how he is legally prohibited from teaching with full acknowledgement that Jesus is the source of all wisdom and knowledge, and in light of how it is possible to obtain a teaching job where one can fully proselytize and grant Jesus His full honor and glory? The Christian Establishment loves to write books about being all in, but when it comes down to it, in American Christendom, it is more fashionable to be Jesus' *secret martyr* than His *open* *ethicist*. To be openly ethical for Jesus draws the standard Christian Establishment accusations I outlined above; being a secret martyr for Jesus is an easier route.

I do not demand that you accept my articulation of the civil government's limits; however, I do expect that you articulate *some* civil government limits. After all, is it not the case that God's church, the *ecclesia*, the body of people walking the earth, have the correct epistemology? Is it not true that God has revealed *what* there is to know, and *how* that knowledge came to be known? In public discourse, in public policy, in public negotiations, this matters: those people externalizing their humanism via civil government must be put on notice that the correct things we are to know (the Bible) hold that they have limits. Those people are suppressing the truth, so how else can we expect them to know what their duties owed to God are unless we tell them? How else can we expect the civil government to know their limits unless we tell them? How else can we expect humanists to know the civil law cannot save unless we tell them? If preachers really know what the source of knowledge is and that the civil government actors are suppressing this fact, how else do preachers expect those civil government actors to know what they are supposed to do as the civil authorities? It is as simple as that. You do not have to agree with what I say the civil government limits are; nevertheless, tell your congregation *something*. In all my church years I have never once heard a preacher espouse civil government limits.

The Christian Establishment tries to justify why they do not discuss how the civil government has limits. Oftentimes preachers will assert that they are not to get political. But if there were no civil government schools, there would still be a need to get political, since we would still need to be proactive in preventing one's establishment.[97] You can see, then, that there is still the need to articulate the civil government's limits so that hypothetical agencies, departments, and so on are never proposed, let alone developed. I have no way of knowing for sure, but I suspect that many preachers find the IRS' existence comforting in that it affords the preacher cover from having to formulate some type of articulable set of civil government principles in the first place. "I am not going to get political here" is the preacher's cover, lest he offend his humanistic congregation.

There is a legitimate reason for espousing civil government limits: limits are biblical. Civil government and politics is within the universe of religion. Public policy can never originate outside of God's universe. There is nowhere to go where God's influence does not reach; it is all under His influence. Preachers nowadays are in full retreat

---

[97] In his book *Is Public Education Necessary?,* Samuel Blumenfeld documents how some early 1800s preachers did, in fact, oppose a civil government school system when one was first being considered and then developed. Samuel L. Blumenfeld, *Is Public Education Necessary?* (Powder Springs, GA: American Vision, 2011).

when it comes to addressing what public policy should be. I concede that a preacher may dip his toe in the water on marriage or abortion. But when was the last time your preacher addressed property taxes (including how church property, like all other property, should be tax exempt)? Or socialism? Compulsory education laws? Again, I do not demand you agree with me on every principle or its application. But it is pitiful how weak the church's articulation is of what civil government should be.

A church's nonprofit exemption status will never be in jeopardy for espousing God's Word on the grounds that everything is theological: is it not theological to assert that property taxes are unbiblical, as God owns everything and we steward to him? That is not political but theological. *But so what if a nonprofit exemption were in jeopardy?* John Knox told Queen Mary right to her face that he would disobey if she conflicted with God.[98] A nonprofit challenge would be an opportune time for the church government to inform the civil government how they are commanded to facilitate the gospel, not interfere with it. You see, the church government's tax exempt status is in direct conflict with the civil government's granting the exemption; it is a worldviews battle. The civil government humanist wants to extinguish the church government Christian. Sometimes I admire humanists; they play to win. The Christian

---

[98] John Knox, *History of the Reformation in Scotland*, (edited by William Croft Dickinson, D.Lit., Philosophical Library, New York, 1950, [in 2 volumes]).

Establishment does not. While it is not the church government's duty owed to God to exercise the power of the physical sword to spread Christianity, it certainly is the church government's duty owed to God to inform the congregation of that fact. That would include condemning the civil government school's existence, and doing so is not a political endeavor, but rather a theological endeavor.

It behooves preachers to reflect on civil government and politics. When we as Christians look at civil government we should see that civil government is a God-ordained institution. Civil government is unique, as the only government where the physical sword's use is justified. Justice is actually the only justified means of using force to "advance" Christianity. If a Christian civil government actor biblically understands what criminal principle was breached, he has the God-given right (via civil government) to enforce (temporal) sanctions on the evildoer. In that situation, the evildoer does not want to be punished; nevertheless, the Christian civil government actor has the God-given right to use the physical sword to enforce the punishment. The reason why I state that justice is actually the only justified means of using force to "advance" Christianity is because there are times where the Christian and humanist are in disagreement (on a public policy level) as to whether there was a criminal principle breached. If the Christian is the civil government actor when a biblical criminal principle is breached, that civil government actor has the right to enforce sanctions, despite what the humanist says. Now, my analysis here does not dispose of every single tangential issue invoked; nevertheless, my point is that the preacher can use Romans 13 as a teaching opportunity: the civil government's duty owed to God is to enforce justice, and enforcing justice involves *force*. In that case, the Christian is justified in "forcing" Christianity on the unregenerate. This is an exciting area of God's Law and is not supposed to embarrass the Christian Establishment preacher.[99]

For at least one more reason, it behooves preachers to reflect on civil government and politics. As I just alluded to, understand what the civil government is: *a mechanism that relies on physical force to apply principles*. Even if you disagree with that brief definition, your definition will hover around it in that it will include how the civil government (to the core) relies on a physical force mechanism to do some things and by deduction *not* do some other things. Then what that mechanism does and does not do requires a line of demarcation, something preachers are loathe to formulate *at all*. Thankfully, so many in American Christendom recognize how Christian Establishment preachers are negligent in this regard, and so those who ignore preachers who refuse to get political should continue in that practice.

---

[99] Per Psalms 2 all civil government leaders shall serve the LORD with fear and rejoice with trembling, not embarrassment.

The civil government's existence is a mechanism that society at large assents to. However, that is not what gives the civil government authority. What gives them authority is Romans 13. But the humanist suppresses the source (Scripture) for there even being a civil government in the first place, and uses that mechanism to advance humanistic causes. This should be, from an apologetic perspective, reason enough to delegitimize the humanist as a civil government actor: he has no ultimate authority, except his own, for applying force and coercion to another. Such is the rationale for the Christian having justification for disobeying the humanist's substantive law to the degree it is repugnant to Scripture.

When the Christian Establishment repeatedly tells American Christendom to refrain from civil government involvement, what results is the pietistic-humanistic alliance so accurately described by so many on the Theonomy side. Preachers *should* exploit this point for all it's worth: *Mr. Humanist, if it were not for Scripture there would not even be such a thing as civil government.* This is where the preacher is inconsistent with the Christian worldview: he wants to say we should refrain from getting political, yet at the same time he will not go so far as to say that civil government should not exist. If we as Christians are to refrain from being the civil government actors, then why should there even be a civil government when the humanists are in power? This is not a straw man argument, but rather it is pushing the antithesis. The

Christian Establishment preacher should adopt the Christian way of thinking about civil government. When Christians refrain from being the civil government, that vacuum is immediately filled by the humanist. The humanist delights in being the civil government because the only thing he has in his arsenal is physical power.

Mind you it is a serious thing how the civil government is a mechanism that justifies one group doing something to another group. For preachers to abdicate exhaustive discussion on the matter, and instead revert to the most superficial analysis and theological hedging, may be gross negligence. I will not beat a dead horse by enumerating all the issues that the preacher could address from a public policy perspective; however, keeping in line with my larger thesis, it is sufficient to point out that the preacher fails to say that the civil government school is a justified use of civil government force. And the fact that he fails in that regard is what is actually causing America's societal decline, insofar as our citizens (regenerate and unregenerate) continue to more and more adopt humanistic principles of morality, societal norms, and civil law.

An ironic point not to be lost in how the Christian Establishment preacher attempts to justify his negligence in espousing civil government limits is that by his dereliction he is actually allowing the Christian to use force and coercion to advance Christianity. Christian Establishment preachers are adamant that we are not to force Christian principles on others, but his refrain from articulating civil government jurisdiction over a child's thoughts allows Christian civil government school teachers to do just that! You see, no matter how much you attempt to suppress otherwise, a Christian civil government school teacher's salary is derived from force and coercion, and their audience members are there by force and coercion. People generally assume that salt and light in the civil government school comes from the student; here, look at it from the employee's perspective: is it not the case that the Christian civil government school employee is using force and coercion to advance Christianity? If he says that he is not advancing Christianity, then he or she is using force and coercion to get paid to tell humanistic lies.

Another reason Christian Establishment preachers use to justify not discussing civil government limits is that supposedly Satan is in charge of that government. Ironically that becomes true if Christians subscribe to such reasoning, as ultimately (and currently) humanists step in to the civil government vacuum as Satan's agents, externalizing his physical sword. However, asserting that Satan is currently in charge of civil government is a theological position, resting on inferences drawn from the biblical texts or a conclusion based on biblical premises. While I am not against biblical inferences or biblical conclusions, it need only be done where necessary; even then it is merely a theological construct and vulnerable as conclusory.

While theological constructs can be biblically deduced, one here does not overcome the express words set forth in Romans 13:3-4:

> For rulers are not a terror to good conduct, but to bad. Would you have no fear of the one who is in authority? Then do what is good, and you will receive his approval, for he is God's servant for your good. But if you do wrong, be afraid, for he does not bear the sword in vain. For he is the servant of God, an avenger who carries out God's wrath on the wrongdoer.

Those two verses qualify how the civil government is not to be a terror to good conduct, but to bad. Know that here I cite Romans 13:3-4, without its context, for the sole purpose of rebutting how the theological construct of the civil government coming under Satan's dominion is supposedly to prevail over the hermeneutical and exegetical understanding of good and bad in Romans 13:3-4. In other words, when someone invokes non-Romans 13 principles and then puts them together to suggest that Satan is in charge of civil government, that is not persuasive enough, nor is it necessary to overcome a Christian's simple biblical perusal of what is good and bad: Satan must not be in charge of the civil government because he is not in the business of promoting good and punishing evildoers—God is.

The advocates of civil government being under Satan's dominion first make the mistake of invoking theology where it is unnecessary, and then they compound the problem by directly contradicting how Romans 13:3-4 describes (propositionally) the civil government as promoting good and punishing evildoers. Again, Satan cannot be the lord over civil government, as he is disqualified in that he is not in the business of promoting good and punishing evildoers; to the contrary, he is in the business of doing the exact opposite, and getting humans—especially the Christian Establishment preacher—to think otherwise. I iterate that when the Christian abdicates civil government on the basis that it falls under Satan's dominion, by direct result of that inaction, the civil government then does fall under Satan's dominion.

Another reason the Christian Establishment uses to justify not discussing the civil government is they say God is in the business of judging the nations through civil government. Ironically, God may be using the civil government to judge the Christian Establishment preacher for not preaching on civil government limits. I do not cite the heavyweights of antiquity to justify my position that the civil government has limits, for I agree with Luther that antiquity is not dispositive of truth.[100] Nevertheless, as I mentioned above, Calvin and so many others have addressed how God judges the nations through civil government. That God uses civil government to judge others does not mean the civil government has unlimited authority, for the authority they have comes from God, and man is not coterminous with God. And it is the case, from what we have seen in world history, God has instituted civil governments that do indeed promote good and punish evildoers. Two examples are the Israelites and their conquest of the Canaanites, and the American colonists, who may have been agents for judging those who worship the Creation over the Creator, and also the English, who were not in conformity with Romans 13. Calvin indeed concluded at the very end of his Institutes:

> [T]hat we are subject to the men who rule over us, but subject only in the Lord. If they command anything against him let us not pay the least regard to it, nor be moved by all the dignity which they possess as magistrates—a dignity to which no injury is done when it is subordinated to the special and truly supreme power of God.[101]

---

[100] Martin Luther, J I. Packer, and O R. Johnston, *The Bondage of the Will* (Grand Rapids: Baker Academic, 1957), 110, note 1.

[101] Calvin and Beveridge, *Institutes of the Christian Religion*, (Grand Rapids, MI: Eerdmans, 1953), 988.

Why is the Christian Establishment preacher so willing to bend over backwards to tell Christians that Romans 13 requires us to be subject to a humanistic civil government, but not willing to lift a finger at analyzing what a Christian civil government should look like?

Understand something more profound, though, in Calvin's *Of Civil Government* analysis, relative to conformity with Romans 13:5: "Therefore one must be in subjection, not only to avoid God's wrath but also for the sake of conscience."[102] That, for conscience' sake, citizens are supposed to obey civil government, and we do so without knowing what the outcome will be of any justified resistance to civil government. What I mean is that man does not know what the future holds; only God has a simultaneous knowledge of the past, present, and future. Thus, whenever we as humans look back on history and cite how God has judged such and such a people, it is only with hindsight; we do not have a present understanding of what future outcome God has ordained for a current situation, which is why, in my estimation, God commands us, for conscience' sake, to be subject to the magistrate he put in place. Only with a clear conscience (that is, where there has been a "long train of abuses" against God) are we justified in disregarding the civil magistrate. We must be sure we are wronged before we are justified in disobeying man for the sake of obeying God.

---

[102] Romans 13:5.

American preachers copy and paste the same old Romans 13 themes. You might think that the copy and paste is a contemporary phenomenon; it is not. The copy and paste has existed for years, and preachers are fond of mimicking what other preachers say on Romans 13. It is not error for us to learn from one another, nor is it error to preach the same thing as someone else. Nevertheless, copying and pasting Romans 13 sermons *ad nauseam* is to American Christendom's detriment.

One copied Romans 13 theme is that in America, "It is not that bad." In other words, you have a car, food on your table, a job that most in the world desire, and a house that is not made of cardboard. "Quit your whining, America", is the refrain. I remember hearing a sermon after Obamacare was legislated that chastised conservatives for complaining about it, as in the United States we still have the best healthcare in the world. But worth quoting is Benjamin Franklin. Not because he was a Framer, but because he seemed to understand proactive externalization of Jesus as Lord: "A republic, if you can keep it" was what he said when prompted after the Constitutional Convention, as to the type of civil government was proposed. You see, just as it takes proactive work in one's private life to keep sin at bay, it takes proactive work in public life to keep tyranny at bay. This is a Christian reality: we must be diligent in being in the Word and we must be diligent in externalizing the Word. But when the preacher presents the copied Romans

13 theme of, "It is not that bad," there is an implied rejection of diligence within the public sphere. Instead he should say, "Obamacare is unbiblical, and here is how I know so..." Then he should extrapolate biblical propositions supporting his position. Instead, he resorts to the amateurish, "It is not that bad."

It seems also to be implied in the common refrain, "It is not that bad," that we are supposed to wait until things get *really bad* in order to take action. "Things are not that bad in America so do not waste your time on reflecting Jesus' lordship in the public sphere, but rather just spend your time telling people Jesus is the Savior." But where in Scripture is there presented this dichotomy of Jesus as Savior or as Lord? God calls all humans to be in His will in different areas of life; that is the body of believers working together—the feet, the hands, the head, and so on. And just as it is the case that we cannot achieve Christian public policy without Christian preaching, we cannot have Christian preaching without Christian public policy, for the humanist wants to quash Christian preaching, and he moves towards that through humanistic public policy. Christians must be involved with public policy, as to not be would be disastrous to advancing the gospel of Jesus Christ. Besides all that, if the Christian Establishment preacher thinks it is not that bad, then are we to wait for his signal to know when it *is* bad? If that is the case, how will he know when things *are* bad? If it is the Bible that will inform him about when to know when things are bad, why not just share that with us now from the pulpit? Then we can try and prevent it!

The family and church governments are complementary. God commands parents to disciple the children, to raise them in His nurture and admonition. This means that God wants each family member to be regenerated, to be His adopted child. So amongst the three governments, from a spiritual perspective, there really are just the church government and civil government. The former works via the spiritual sword and the latter the physical sword. But both must be Christian led, as then the gospel flourishes. The gospel flourishes when the church government is preaching and teaching how fathers are in charge of raising children in the Lord's nurture and admonition. That preaching and teaching must include not just the affirmative that fathers are in charge of teaching the Christian worldview, but also the negative that fathers are to do this to the exclusion of the civil government. In other words, both the affirmative and the negative legs must exist, otherwise the body cannot move forward; it goes in a circle. It is not supposed to go in a circle; it is supposed to march forward.

Suggesting we wait until things get really bad in the public sphere before we take action is a disastrous idea, as there then would not even be the public outlet for preachers to proclaim anything Christian; how then would that allow humans to be vessels to advance God's Kingdom? It is not a sin to be involved with civil government and politics, as long as the person is within the civil government's God-ordained jurisdiction. The politician is doing just as much to facilitate and advance the gospel when he correctly implements and preserves public policy that allows the preacher to preach and the father to teach. To say otherwise is to disavow a connection between what our theology is and what we do on an everyday operational basis. I bravely and confidently assert that God's Kingdom advances mightily in the face of opposition, but nowadays the opposition is not the humanistic civil government; it is the Christian Establishment. The Christian Establishment has it all wrong. We are in the public sphere working towards Christian public policy, which if reflective of Romans 13, facilitates the gospel. We are not without the gospel, as we know that Jesus is not just the Savior, but the Lord over everything, including civil government. We are doing our job; you are not doing yours, and you undercut us when you say that Christians should not be involved with politics.

The only way the Christian Establishment preacher can continue to do his job in the long run is if he espouses the biblical proposition that we must do ours politically. When Christians are the civil government actors, while there will not be perfection, we can expect a society that properly executes justice. We can also expect that all other areas of life have the potential to be facilitated just as they should—by families and churches. That is the whole reason for the conservative claim that there should be small civil government, because the civil government should be merely that which is articulated in Scripture: promote good (facilitate duties owed to God) and punish evildoers (execute justice where one interferes with another's duties owed to God). Conservatism is what it is because of Romans 13.

When Christians are the civil government, they understand that the civil government is not what is special; the pulpit is what is special, because it proclaims the gospel of Jesus as Savior and Lord. When Christians are the civil government, they understand that man, via the civil government, is not exalted; Jesus is exalted. When Christians are the civil government, they understand that man is not the ultimate authority; Jesus is the ultimate authority, and He is a big God in whom all is vested, including lordship over civil government.

As I alluded to, another copied Romans 13 theme is that Christians are not supposed to be involved with civil government, as that diverts resources from the gospel. I am not going to repeat the common arguments about Romans, because there is a standoff between the Christian Establishment on the one hand and the numeric minority of people that are to me like-minded. Nevertheless, at the debate center there tends to be dispute as to what Jesus meant when he said, "Render to Caesar the things that are Caesar's, and to God the things that are God's."[103] That saying says more about the human

---

[103] Matthew 22:21.

unpacking it than Jesus' teaching, because Jesus was allowing the audience to opine about what belongs to Caesar and what belongs to God. Thus, the correct way for the Christian to unpack that passage is that everything, including coinage and the faith that gives it value, belongs to God. Jesus has authority over all, comporting with how Christians are supposed to be involved with civil government. There is comportment because Jesus has authority over Caesar—the civil government. It is to Jesus that we are to render all things.

Now hopefully you understand that an unfortunate consequence to the assertion that Christians are not supposed to be involved with politics suffers the gospel. The Christian Establishment preacher condemns Jesus as Lord over the civil government ruling vicariously through man and, when American Christendom listens to them, the gospel suffers. Preachers condemn using resources to facilitate biblical civil government when, in fact, resources are *not* used to facilitate biblical civil government. In the long run, those resources are taken from us Christians to be used for humanistic purposes, as humanists fill the vacuum created by Christians; the vacuum is filled with humanistic policy that moves to eliminate the opposition. For example, through the Sixteenth Amendment the federal civil government has the "legal" power to tax us at one hundred percent.[104] In that regard a tax

---

[104] The Congress shall have power to lay and collect taxes on incomes, from whatever source derived, without

even remotely close to that percentage proportionately prevents the congregant from fulfilling his duties owed to God—including the biblical command to pay our preachers. With that example preachers should learn very quickly that the governments are a zero sum.

Preachers are fond of picking on Christians involved with civil government. They copy and paste but never take an honest, intellectual look away from their little god and at the big picture, so they do not see that God's big picture includes physically protecting the gospel He wants articulated. Is it really true that God revealed to us that the preferred situation is that civil governments become tyrannical, so as to prohibit evangelism? Has God revealed to us that He wants us to be martyred by a humanistic civil government, rather than be leaders via the civil government? Has God revealed to us that He wants us to be secret agents of how Jesus is mere Savior, but not public delegates of the full gospel message that Jesus is the Lord?

Understand that Jesus' civil government lordship is not for the purpose of merely making the best of humanistic situations. Rather, it is for facilitating the full gospel message so that people can spend eternity enjoying God. Oddly, if we are not to deal with civil government, then one forfeits a call for prayer for missionaries in foreign lands being

---

apportionment among the several states, and without regard to any census or enumeration (*U.S. Constitution*, Amend. XVI).

persecuted by humanist tyrants. Christians and our preachers are to articulate and implement proper civil government in this nation so that others can learn what the Bible says about God's universal laws.

Another copied Romans 13 theme is that we are to absolutely pay taxes. Romans 13:6-7 informs us:

> For because of this you also pay taxes, for the authorities are ministers of God, attending to this very thing. Pay to all what is owed to them: taxes to whom taxes are owed, revenue to whom revenue is owed, respect to whom respect is owed, honor to whom honor is owed.

The Christian Establishment glosses right over how it is expressly stated in that passage why we pay taxes: "For because of this" ("this" meaning that the civil government is supposed to promote good and punish evildoers). In Romans 13:6-7 we are specifically told *why* we pay taxes.

Glossing over Romans 13:6-7 is perhaps the biggest Christian Establishment blunder. In the Romans 13 passage is first the explanation about civil authority submission, as if we are submitting to God. Second is that we are submitting to civil government actors who are promoting good and punishing evildoers. And third is the explanation for why we pay taxes.

In light of the very easily understandable Romans 13, why is the Christian Establishment's Romans 13 theme: *Obey what the civil government commands and pay them what they demand!*[105]

From the Christian Establishment preacher there is virtually no analysis how verses three and four qualify the civil government's duties owed to God, or how in verse six we are instructed as to why we pay taxes. Understand that the civil government is a type of minister of God; that is why we are commanded to pay them. In failing to articulate why we are to pay taxes, the preacher opens the door for socialism, which is the forced extraction of tax dollars from one group to be given to another group. But unfortunately the preacher's message is that, if a tax is levied then you owe it, even if it goes beyond the civil government's jurisdiction of promoting good and punishing evildoers.

Many preachers have a twisted view on unpacking Scripture: when it comes to what we may do as Christians, that means whatever is *not* prohibited in the New Testament; but when it comes to what we may do with civil government, that means whatever Jesus *did not do* relative to the civil government. Does that make any sense to you? I know Jesus spoke in parables, but even parables do not require such mental gymnastics. It is true that Jesus did not run for office during his earthly stint, but if the preacher is going to say that we may do whatever is

---

[105] That could be the Christian Establishment's Romans 13 hymn.

not prohibited in the New Testament, then that means Christians may run for office. If the Christian Establishment preacher condemns Christians for civil government involvement, then that requires him to condemn civil government school teachers.

When we look at Scripture we must know that it speaks to all life's areas. So if the preacher asserts that Jesus did not speak to civil government, the Bible somewhere does. I think the Bible speaks to civil government in Romans 13 and other parts of even just the New Testament. And there is something profound in Scripture that speaks to civil government, and that is that the physical sword is for imperfect temporal justice, and, in conjunction, the spiritual sword is for perfect eternal peace with God. That is why Christians are to participate in civil government, because only the Christian knows the difference. Romans 13 is not salvific, but only the Christian knows that, and so Christians must be the civil government actors to prevent humanists from implementing their version of salvation.

Through Romans 13 negligence, the Christian Establishment disengages the humanist's church, the civil government school system, negatively affecting the gospel.

CHRISTIAN FREEDOM

The law and gospel issue will not be settled here, but in the course of explaining the Christian

Establishment's deficiencies on Christian Freedom, it is a good idea to explain to you what I think is the correct way to view Scripture.

I do not think the Mosaic Law was designed to save. That is, I do not agree with the following statement: *It is not that the Mosaic Law cannot save, it is that we cannot keep that Law*. I think one was saved prior to God's incarnation the same way he is saved after God's incarnation: by putting his faith in God as the Savior and Lord and, thereafter, being regenerated via the Holy Ghost. Any law revealed to us was and is to expose our need for regeneration and sanctification, not to be a means for salvation. Looking at it that way matters because it affects what one does with revealed law, especially the law set down in the Scriptures prior to Jesus' time on Earth. In other words, now that Jesus came and died for our sins, it does not mean that law is here and gone—disregarded because it is no longer salvific.[106]

To assert that the law remains, subject to Jesus' interpretation of it, I think, is to merely assert that principles remain. Again, I do not think the law was ever designed to save; I think it was given to show us how to live, that we are sinners in need of a Savior or further sanctification. It all boils down to how we still have principles that guide our everyday lives; we can still look back to the Mosaic Law—and other principles—and rely on them.

---

[106] I do believe the Mosaic Law's ceremonial laws have been "put out of gear" as they say.

Within the umbrella of law and gospel there is the discussion about a hierarchy of principles (1 Corinthians 15:1-4), the weightier matters of the law (Matthew 23:23-24), and Christian Freedom relating to ceremonial law (Romans 14).[107] And there is the discussion about what we now are to do with Old Testament law (1 Timothy 1:7-8). These discussions are not necessarily mutually exclusive.

What someone thinks of God's purpose for revealing principles matters threefold. First, it means that someone who holds to a similar perspective (as me) on law and gospel cannot be accused of perpetuating works-based religion. I iterate this because the Christian Establishment preacher oftentimes confuses *work* with *works*. He sees someone like me working hard, hustling, trying to advance the gospel, getting dirty, and he thinks that I am works-based. He confuses *work* with *works*.

Second, the Christian Establishment preacher thinks reconstructing society to reflect biblical principles is *worldliness*, and that that is inferior to being a *spiritual* vessel in this *physical* world. Only God is privy to know the difference when one is acting according to the former or the latter, as only He can "see" motive. But it is possible that one is a civil government actor who, because he has been regenerated by the spiritual sword, is a spiritual vessel in this physical world, limiting civil

---

[107] This discussion is inapplicable here.

government to promoting good and punishing evildoers. That is not *worldliness*; it is *worldview*. Speaking of worldliness, the Christian Establishment preacher should try externalizing Christianity some time, in the real world. He would be lost without principles, for Christian Freedom does not mean there are no applicable principles.

And third, so crucially, principles give us an anchor. Yes, Jesus is the anchor, as fulfillment of the law. But all that is to say that we are to emulate Jesus; we are to aim for being like Jesus in thought and action; we are to mimic Jesus. Lest you think that is preaching to the choir (for who would reject such a thing?), I raise that point because it would be absurd that a preacher would not talk about mimicking Jesus.[108] What I mean is, would it not be improper if we did not talk about Jesus simply because we could not be like him? Of course it would be improper; likewise, it is improper to not talk about what civil government should be, even if we will never perfectly achieve it.

Disregarding principles, though, is biblically improper because it causes Christians to degrade into something of a relativism, as some divide the Word into a hierarchy of principles, with Dogma[109]

---

[108] Matthew 5:17 interpretation is at the center of debate between two basic schools of thought on the relationship between law and gospel. But how can someone claim on the one hand that Jesus fulfilled the law, but on the other hand claim we should not then talk about how to be like Jesus as the fulfillment of the law?

[109] 1 Corinthians 15:1-4; Galatians 1:6.

at the top, Doctrine[110] below it, and, thereafter, Conviction[111] and then Preference.[112]

The reason I include the hierarchy of principles discussion in the Christian Freedom discussion is that by solely focusing on 1 Corinthians 15:1-4 as our Christian core, the Christian Establishment discounts everything, including law, thereafter. In other words, it basically puts everything outside of 1 Corinthians 15:1-4 in play as acceptable in belief or practice. It is the lowest common denominator of Christianity, and it disregards how one would even know (by the law) he sinned, requiring a savior in the first place. Never mind how Paul wrote his letter because there were lies within the church: the prohibition against lying is in itself not, according to the Christian Freedom proponent, apparently a dogma or doctrine, but rather a conviction or preference.

The threshold reason the Christian Establishment preacher is in error classifying the discussion of the civil government school's existence as conviction or preference is that he assumes that what is in dispute is delegation, not jurisdiction. That he does so is at the peril of souls under his care. He thinks ultimately that the conversation is about whether to delegate a child's education to the civil government, but as I have stated many times over, the real issue is whether there should be civil government schools

---

[110] 1 Thessalonians 4:17.
[111] 1 Corinthians 8:4-13; Romans 14:13-23.
[112] 1 Corinthians 7:6.

in the first place; the real issue is whether lies are being told and whether we are facilitating those lies with our money and children; the real issue is whether the civil government has jurisdiction over the heart and mind. The jurisdiction issue makes the delegation issue moot.

I do not think the delegation issue should be categorized as a conviction or preference. Nevertheless, granting for argument's sake that it could be, there is still no cover for the preacher *not* addressing whether a civil government school's existence is biblically proper, as Romans 13 leaves no room for their existence being considered a personal conviction or preference. Moreover, if the civil government may use force and coercion to advance thought, what power can the Christian Establishment preacher cite as a retort to what they *cannot* do? But more pointedly, is it really the case that it is a matter of conviction or preference that the civil government operate civil government schools? How we react to them (*delegation*) might be; but not whether they exist (*jurisdiction*). And when Jesus spoke about the weightier matters of the law, he did not invert the Pharisaic model of more important and less important; rather, he states that *all* of it is important: "These [the weightier matters of the law—justice and mercy and faith] you ought to have done, without neglecting the others."[113]

Christian Freedom discussions are not necessarily mutually exclusive. Consider all that with the

---

[113] Matthew 23:23.

hierarchy of principles discussion and also the discussion about the interaction between the Old and New Testaments. I challenge you to circumvent your Christian Establishment preacher and consider how the biblical argument against civil government schools is tighter than the biblical argument against abortion. That is not to say that I do not think the argument against abortion is lock tight; it is. But why is it that when we come to the abortion issue we cite the Old Testament? We cite Jeremiah 1:5 and Psalms 139 and Isaiah 49:1; we cite Genesis 1 and how man is made in God's image; we cite the sixth commandment. But Christians cite the Old Testament (partially) because there is no express abortion prohibition in the New Testament. I ask, in the interest of iron sharpening iron: How can one think abortion is wrong when there is no New Testament provision prohibiting such a thing?

So oftentimes what is in the Old Testament is brazenly dismissed as applicable only to Israel.[114] And we are told, *The New Testament does not prohibit that, so it is okay ... Christian Freedom.* Again, I do not think that abortion is biblically justified. I am merely pressing those who claim that there must be an express New Testament prohibition for something to be improper, or otherwise it falls under Christian Freedom.

Still further I ask, in still challenging you, because your preacher has never done so: To what degree

---

[114] "Should Christians Send Their Kids to Public Schools? *Up For Debate*. Moody Radio. WMBI, Chicago. 6 June 2014.

must a Greek sentence in the New Testament match what we need it to say in order for it to provide contemporary instruction? That is a legitimate question! It is so legitimate, in fact, that it could decide whether abortion is or is not proper (according to the person who claims that something in contemporary times is acceptable merely because it is not prohibited in the New Testament). To what degree must the Greek words match a contemporary application? What if the Bible outlawed a "strip club" but not a "gentlemen's club"? Would the latter be prohibited? More insistently, this does not dispose of qualifying abortion as what is translated as *murder* in Matthew 19:18; one would still need to qualify abortion as murder.

I think abortion is murder and I think murder is prohibited, but not because of the New Testament. And I also think that it is good practice to invoke Old Testament principles, for they are (generally) still binding. So it is not that I think the Christian is wrong in invoking the Old Testament to show how abortion is wrong; but I am showing here how inconsistent the Christian Establishment is with murder and lying: for the former it is acceptable to cite the Old Testament to qualify abortion as murder; for the latter it is unacceptable to cite any part of Scripture to disqualify the civil government school teacher's employ. Whether a Christian is taxed so that a teacher can tell humanistic lies is not a matter of conviction or preference.

Classifying the delegation issue as conviction or preference degrades Christianity, to some degree, into relativism, which exists when people create their own principles. *Do not impute your preferences on me!* But the Bible covers all areas of life, so there are no situations where the Bible does not invoke principles—either expressly or logically. Besides, even though I concede that there is a hierarchy of principles, how could one possibly consider the matter of the civil government discipling our children to be void of any applicable principles, or to be a matter of conviction or preference? Are you not, as a civil government school teacher, imputing your convictions and preferences onto the home school teacher via your salary, derived from taxes? Are you not, as a civil government school teacher, telling young impressionable minds what you think truth is?

One could quite easily extrapolate the Ten Commandments and find sins relating to false idols, sexual immorality, stealing (via taxation), and lying, and come to the conclusion that preferences and convictions are imputed on the Christian student and Christian taxpayer—everyday! Yet the Christian Establishment never changes, and they are hypocritical in that *they* are not willing to tell their congregations the things they expect children, as vessels, to articulate in civil government schools.

Through Christian Freedom the Christian Establishment disengages the humanist's church, the civil government school system, negatively affecting the gospel.

END-TIMES SPECULATION

Despite how one literally has no way of knowing it is the case, many in the Christian Establishment make American Christendom indifferent to externalizing Christianity by claiming that Jesus' return to earth is imminent or a rapture is imminent. This causes American Christendom to disengage society, as it is a supposed waste of time to take the medium- to long-term approach to working towards societal norms and civil law reflecting biblical principles. Many in the Christian Establishment, by preaching Jesus' imminent return, lull American Christendom into unnecessarily believing that taking the time to externalize Christianity in all areas of life is not a good use of Christian resources. They claim that Jesus is coming back soon and, therefore, expending the energy to implement Christian societal norms and civil laws is inconsistent with how we now are supposed to live.

Christians are inherently forward-looking though. We have an ongoing concern that affects our present behavior. We save money for a child's college fund and for retirement, we exercise, we partake in Bible studies and build relationships, and we maintain our homes and cars. Would any of that be necessary if Jesus' return were imminent? The Christian Establishment is inconsistent in this regard: would a church leader not pay his church's mortgage if it extends out more than thirteen years? (Thirteen being the number of civil government school system academic years.)

In the Christian Establishment exists the assumption that the way to save society is to save individuals and, therefore, a mandate advancing Christian principles is a waste of time. It is a waste of time because Jesus is coming back, and when He does, He is only going to be concerned about who is and who is not saved—not whether societal norms and civil law reflect Jesus. A society that reflects Jesus, it is thought, is irrelevant, and one that does reflect Jesus was for naught because, again, the only thing that matters is whether someone is saved.

Oftentimes parents just want to accept the humanistic paradigms we have in our society, and then justify operating within those paradigms with, "Well, Jesus is coming back soon so it will not matter." But if you knew that Jesus had already come back, He was not coming back for a long time, or you were commanded not to be worried about His return, would it not prompt you to do more about society reflecting Christian principles? Instead, many lazily assert, "I am not going to bother starting a Christian school because it is too much work in the face of the humanist onslaught, and, besides, Jesus is coming back soon, so it will not matter anyway."

Hidden in the assertion that Jesus' return is imminent is an epistemological premise. Epistemology is the study of knowledge, or more specifically, what it is we know and how it is we come to know it. For the Christian, our way of knowing things is through God's Revelation to us. That is, we can only know things about God's Creation and about His nature because He has revealed to us knowledge about those things. Otherwise we would know nothing. For millenniums, humans autonomously pondering philosophy (ethics, metaphysics, and epistemology) have stumbled in the dark and have been unable to refute Christianity, let alone come away with a satisfactory, comprehensive view of life.[115] All this is to say that when the Christian Establishment preacher asserts that Jesus is coming back soon, he is claiming to *know* that is the case. Anyone claiming to actually know that Jesus' return is imminent holds the burden of overcoming how Jesus Himself stated in Matthew 24:36 that only the Father knows when Jesus will return. And who are we as humans to inquire about what only God the Father is said to know?

I know of no Christian who claims to know, based on a *personal revelation* from God, that Jesus' return is imminent. In that case, the only way of (allegedly) knowing His return is imminent is by looking at the world and determining if the environment that exists matches the biblical clues

---

[115] Luther, Packer, and Johnston, *The Bondage of the Will*, 121.

that supposedly indicate when Jesus is supposed to return. But it is still only an *argument* to assert that Jesus' return is imminent.

Whether Jesus returns after another two thousand years, thirteen years, or ten minutes, it is not only the case that we will not know, but we must continue to occupy God's field and do business until the actual return. The return is said to be analogous to what happened in Noah's days: people did not expect what happened. That makes it even more crucial that we understand that now is the time to be born again, for we know not how long Jesus will tarry His return. But this does not mean a withdrawal from externalizing Christianity in the form of societal norms and civil law; on the contrary, it makes those things more important to be in existence, for they make for a constant witness to the unregenerate. Besides all that, would it not be the case that Jesus' imminent return requires a child's immediate civil government school withdrawal?

End-times speculation wastes resources. Think of how many Christians operate infrastructure, dedicated in part or whole, to speculating on Jesus' return. What that infrastructure does is monitor current events and fit them into the Bible, what I heard through different channels that the late Greg L. Bahnsen called "newspaper exegesis." The downfall to all the wasted effort in speculating on Jesus' supposed imminent return is that it neutralizes those who may want to begin projects that require an enormous amount of time and energy to accomplish. It convinces some to put in abeyance engaging society, and it can have the effect of reducing one's day to day Christian operation to a nihilism of sorts, as societal and political institutions are deemed worthless. We are spiraling downwards, so why bother to build Christian infrastructure?

It is furthermore unproductive to even speculate on Jesus' return, as to so many it becomes pure and simple entertainment. The humanist experiences excitement in implementing his societal and civil paradigms, displacing Christian paradigms. But the Christian, even with hope in Jesus and armed with a spiritual sword that is greater than a physical sword, refuses to look forward to a Christian society. The withdrawal, due to unnecessary end-times speculation, preoccupies the Christian, as he is now distracted with consuming this speculation as entertainment, instead of being spurred on to positively affect societal norms and civil law for the gospel's sake. Meanwhile, humanists are occupying the field Christians are not, based on this end-times speculation withdrawal. That means in the battle of externalizing worldviews, when the humanist externalizes his worldview, we do not counter with externalizing Christianity; instead, we counter the humanist's external advances by citing Jesus' supposed return. This boils down to the Christian's rallying cry being *defeat*, *retreat*, and then *repeat.*[116] Obviously this is not in accord with the Great Commission.

In the societal battle between humanism and Christianity, the humanist outworkings must be met with Christian outworkings. So, it is not the case that the humanist outworkings relative to societal norms and civil law should be met with our merely citing the Holy Ghost; rather, they should be met with our outworkings relative to societal norms and civil law, *powered* by the Holy Ghost. This sets up the real showdown between God's spiritual power and man's physical power. In that vein, as the Christian Establishment wants to disregard Christians (God forbid) externalizing societal norms and civil law, and *merely* invoke Jesus and His supposed imminent return, they fully ignore the prospect that we already have all the power we need in God's Holy Ghost.

When someone like me comes along and broaches civil government school abolition, it blows a fat hole in the claim that we are supposed to withdraw from society, in light of Jesus' supposed imminent return; it blows a fat hole in the claim that we are to defeat, retreat, and repeat. While it is true that my view calls for a medium- to long-term view on life (as abolition and the replacement of the current infrastructure will, of course, take time), abolition is not exclusively a medium- to long-term view. That is because civil government school abolition is

---

[116] DeMar and North, *Christian Reconstruction: What It Is, What It Isn't*, 70.

only possible when family government and church government education increases; and it does not take the medium- to long-term to accomplish many forms of Christian education. Homeschooling is the obvious example, as it can be accomplished, along with the necessary accommodations, in a relatively short period of time. That is not only a successful rebuttal against the defeat, retreat, and repeat proponent; it is also a rebuttal against the Christian Establishment preacher who really believes Jesus' return is imminent, as it prompts him to preach *immediate extraction* from the humanistic civil government schools, in favor of the gospel being evangelized to all American children.

Taking the medium- to long-term view to evangelism is impliedly discouraged through end-times speculation, making abolition unpalatable. Look back through history though at how many times God's people have been wrong about something important. The Jews are the obvious example in that they missed how Jesus is the Messiah. Paul, too, as, if it were not for God's intervention he would have been eternally dead wrong. Throughout the ages, of course with the benefit of hindsight and someone pushing the antithesis, we have come through as a stronger, more galvanized body of believers. Obviously the Protestant Reformation comes to mind too.

End-times speculation is big business though, and even if not done with the intent to neutralize Christian outworkings, it nevertheless has that effect. Check your favorite Christian bookstore and you will see that the books speculating on Jesus' return are more numerous than works outlining how Christian presuppositions apply to societal norms and civil law. Indeed, go to your favorite Christian retailer's website and search "end times" versus "dominion." The amount of time it takes to write end-times books and the amount of time wasted reading them restrain the gospel. End-times *speculation* is actually end-times *sensationalism*, and it seems to be designed more to please the human with *preoccupation* rather than please God with *occupation*.

Jesus wants us to occupy until His return.[117] Establishing societal norms and civil law, with Jesus as the anchor to it all, is just the body of Christ working together: some do this, some do that; some are called to emphasize personal morality, some societal norms, and some civil law. But we all work together. That means it is not the case that just because some Christians are involved with civil law that they are trying to change society from the top down or via legislation. The fact that the Christian Establishment thinks that shows how little they understand those of us who fully extend Jesus' purview; it shows how withdrawn they are from engaging society.

Unfortunately, Christians, instead of occupying, ignore Jesus' words and subscribe to the mantra of defeat, retreat, and repeat. That means every time

---

[117] Luke 19:13.

humanism advances further into the Christian church, the Christians accept the defeat and further retreat, hoping the humanists will leave us alone. Humanists know this is a battle with one winner and one loser, and they play to win. Even though civil government schools are a church that expressly competes with the Christian church, Christians naively think that Christian education and humanistic education can coexist. They cannot; *one will abolish the other*. Christians, on the basis that they see no problem with a civil government school's existence, pass this mentality down to the generations, sometimes led by the idea that Jesus' return is imminent.

End-times speculation is the Christian Establishment's assertion that we are not to *occupy*; instead, we are to be *preoccupied* with the fascination about Jesus' return. The Christian Establishment preacher often delivers a sermon (absent a gospel presentation) alleging that Jesus is coming back soon, so we need not bother polishing brass on a sinking ship.[118] Thus, instead of American Christendom assuming leadership positions, we are to allow societal and civil defeat, retreat in the hopes humanists have gained enough, and then repeat, as the Christian Establishment has not learned the lesson. After each defeat we are to use that lost ground as evidence that Jesus is coming back soon. After all, since things are getting worse that means Jesus' return is imminent.

---

[118] The question "Why polish brass on a sinking ship?" is generally attributed to the late Dr. J. Vernon McGee.

The problem with the mentality that we are not to occupy, but to be preoccupied, is it is a losing mentality. It abandons acting like a Christian and advancing God's Kingdom; it acts as an excuse to operate like a humanist in forcefully taking others' money and compelling their appearance at a civil government school. In like manner, it emasculates the man, and takes from him the mandate to *take* action; instead he sits home and plays video games. Quite honestly I have no problem with someone having a different end times viewpoint. But when the person disengages societal norms and civil law, that is a serious problem. Besides, why is what happens here in America determinant as to the entire world's condition, and Jesus' return?

To question end-times speculation is to question the Christian Establishment, analogous to an American questioning why we are involved with such and such a war: it suggests a lack of patriotism, or that one is not a team player. The Christian Establishment does not like to be questioned, and they have primed American Christendom to marginalize people like me.

To be fair, this problem is not entirely the Christian Establishment's fault; American Christendom shares in this problem in that many Christians would rather be sensationalized by the speculation of Jesus' return, as if being held in anticipation gives something exciting to look forward to. Many Christians would rather be tantalized by predictions amid the usually foreign outbreak of chaos and mass destruction—the supposed end-times signs. Being distracted by such chaos and mass destruction is often an excuse for not advancing the Kingdom of God, an excuse for water cooler talk and not advancing Jesus' lordship.

Exercising Christian leadership takes not hours, but decades. And as stated above, private education and abolition are two sides of the same coin. So not only do people not want to work on abolition, simultaneously they do not want to work on private education. After all, training a child in righteousness does not take hours, it takes years. But as Jesus is supposed to return soon, why bother?

Through end-times speculation the Christian Establishment disengages the humanist's church, the civil government school system, negatively affecting the gospel.

DISOBEDIENCE TO JESUS AS LORD OVER ALL

While on vacation in 2008 I read Supreme Court Justice Clarence Thomas's autobiography, *My Grandfather's Son*. In that book and regarding an experience he had while an undergraduate at Holy Cross he writes:

> During my second week on campus, I went to Mass for the first and last time at Holy Cross. I don't know

why I bothered—probably habit, or guilt—but whatever the reasons, I got up and walked out midway through the homily. It was all about Church dogma, not the social problems with which I was obsessed, and seemed to me hopelessly irrelevant.[119]

On that same vacation, providentially, the very next book I read was John Piper's *Finally Alive*. If you can believe it, in that book Piper cites Clarence Thomas above, and then in response he writes this:

So in any given worship service a dozen young, idealistic Clarence Thomases might be present, full of anger about racism, or global warming, or abortion, or limited health care for children, or homelessness, or poverty, or the war in Iraq, or white-collar crime, or human trafficking, or the global AIDS crisis, or rampant fatherlessness, or the greed behind the sub-prime mortgage crisis, or the treatment of illegal aliens, or the plight of Christians just coming out of prison. And then they hear me announce that today we are going to talk about the way a person can be

---

[119] Clarence Thomas, *My Grandfather's Son*, (New York: Harper Perennial, 2007), 51.

born again. And they might react like Clarence Thomas did and simply walk out and say, "That has nothing to do with the real problems this world is facing."

… They would be wrong—doubly wrong. They would be wrong, in the first place, in failing to see that what Jesus meant by the new birth is supremely relevant for racism and global warming and abortion and health care and all the other issues of our day. … And they would be wrong, secondly, in thinking that those issues are the most important issues in life. They aren't. They are life-and-death issues. But they are not the most important, because they deal with the relief of suffering during this brief earthly life, not the relief of suffering during the eternity that follows. Or to put it positively, they deal with how to maximize well-being now for eighty years or so, but not with how to maximize well-being in the presence of God for eighty trillion years and more.

I think John Piper misunderstood Clarence Thomas. Clarence Thomas was not frustrated with Jesus the Savior, but with how the Christian Establishment fails to connect Jesus to everyday life as Lord. Once a person is regenerated, that same Holy Spirit compels him to externalize Christianity in all spheres, affecting all of the enumerated issues above. But the Christian Establishment reduces Christianity to personal morality, mimicking Jesus, to the exclusion of societal norms and civil law.

It is my contention that it is not Clarence Thomas's God that is the problem; it is the Establishment's. The new birth *should* affect everything done thereafter. That is not to say that sanctification comes immediately. Every Christian is moved along by God's Holy Spirit in different ways and times. But, as Piper implied, the new birth *should* affect everything. But that is as far as the Christian Establishment is willing to go. And because that is as far as they are willing to go, American Christendom is not properly externalizing Christianity in *every* area of life, and, therefore, evangelism is negatively affected.

Piper's book is about regeneration; and in it, regarding regeneration, there is not a single word I disagree with. I am thankful he wrote the book, and when possible I use it as an evangelism tool, supplementing Scripture. My point in quoting him at length is to show how the Christian Establishment perpetuates a worldview application vacuum. It is correct that what is of supreme importance is regeneration. However, in abandoning how to apply the Christian worldview to everyday life post-regeneration (sanctification),

American Christendom's evangelism efforts have been truncated.

Piper's list, in which is not enumerated a biblical civil government, is not for maximizing well-being now or even trying to minimize suffering during this brief earthly life. It is about showing people they are sinners in need of a Savior. It is about the gospel—Jesus as Savior *and* Lord over all. And the gospel is about spending eighty trillion years or more enjoying God.

Certainly regeneration is of supreme importance. Who would argue with that? But why is there then this false dichotomy between preaching the new birth on the one hand, or on the other hand how to go out into God's Creation and externalize it? Why is it the case that each and every sermon does not first talk about the new birth *and* then how to externalize it into one of the enumerated issues? Preaching about the new birth to the exclusion of how to harness that new birth is an insult to Jesus' lordship. The sermon essentially becomes a truncated presentation of Jesus' Saviorship for, at most, a handful of unregenerate people in the congregation, instead of a full presentation of Jesus' Saviorship and then how to externalize it through obedience to Jesus as Lord; it becomes a presentation at the lowest common denominator.

I think Piper misunderstood what Thomas was saying; it was not that Thomas wanted to achieve utopia in the United States,[120] but rather it was that he wanted to see a connection between God putting faith in us as humans and it externalized through us in life. Granted, I cannot know for sure exactly what Thomas meant; to be fair to me, though, neither can Piper know for sure exactly what Thomas meant. Only God can know for sure what Thomas meant. Even so, Piper conceded that the new birth should affect everything, yet the Christian Establishment still presents a truncated gospel. Despite what may have been or still are Thomas's flaws in Roman Catholic theology, I completely understand his frustration.

In innumerable ways one could analyze Piper's enumerated issues and connect the new birth with externalizing the gospel. That too holds true for civil government: they must be Christian, so that others see how regenerated people go about infusing the gospel into all areas of life. Do you see this false dichotomy of regeneration and what it compels? The Christian Establishment may be partially responsible for driving young people to the (amorphous) Emergent Church, for how big could the Christian God be if He does not touch reality? Regeneration causes us to reach out everywhere— not for minimizing temporal earthly pain, but for maximizing eternal heavenly joy.

---

[120] I say sarcastically that, based on Justice Thomas' legal decisions, he is definitely not trying to achieve a Christian utopia.

It seems to me that announcing how today's sermon is about how a person can be born again should always be connected with how we go about everyday business—like making judicial decisions! If preachers connected regeneration with everyday life, there may not have ever evolved the Emergent Church, some of whom do not even know (like Clarence Thomas was able to identify) why they walked out.

In the 1990s there was a debate about what is generally termed "Lordship Salvation." The debate was about whether a person's regeneration means either acknowledging Jesus as Savior, or whether a person's regeneration means acknowledging Jesus as Savior *and* as Lord. So, in one camp there were those who asserted that a regenerated person has only Jesus as Savior, and that obedience to Jesus as Lord is subsequent to, and not simultaneous to, regeneration; and in the other camp were those who asserted that a regenerated person has Jesus as Savior and Lord. The latter camp, into which John MacArthur falls and with which I agree, holds that a person cannot acknowledge Jesus as Savior without simultaneously acknowledging Him as Lord. Here I mainly take issue with those who fall into MacArthur's camp, for the former group is inclusive.

In the Introduction to John MacArthur's book *The Gospel According to Jesus*, Pastor MacArthur writes: "The gospel in vogue today holds forth a false hope to sinners. It promises them they can have eternal life yet continue to live in rebellion to God. Indeed, it encourages people to claim Jesus as Savior yet defer until later the commitment to obey Him as Lord."[121] When I first heard that MacArthur wrote a book about Jesus' lordship I was ecstatic. After all, American Christendom, in my estimation, is currently suffering from the mere observance that Jesus is Savior. That is why I was excited to read MacArthur's book; the subject matter is wholly crucial to American Christendom's crisis.

Yet still, many in the Christian Establishment, even with the correct view that Jesus is to the regenerated person Savior *and* Lord, have a truncated view of Jesus as Lord, which is that obedience to our Lord is not in *all* areas of life, but rather in merely spreading the message that Jesus is the Savior. Do you see the problem with this thinking? Some parents send a child to a civil government school for evangelistic purposes on the grounds that the child is to tell others about Jesus being the Savior. Under this mentality, the child is supposedly obedient to Jesus as Lord because he is telling others about how Jesus is the Savior. No other obedience to Jesus the Lord is required under that truncated lordship mentality.

Full biblical obedience to our Lord accounts for how some parents privately educate a child, hoping that he or she learns how the Bible applies to *all* areas of life. Thereafter, the child is able to tell

---

[121] John MacArthur Jr., *The Gospel According to Jesus*, (Grand Rapids: Zondervan, 1989), 15.

others about Jesus being sent to save us, and how subsequent obedience to him is manifested in *all* areas of life, not just telling others about how Jesus is the Savior. Under this mentality, the child is obedient to Jesus as Lord because he is telling others about how Jesus is the Messiah *and* Lord over all, including the civil government. This is how Christianity is perpetuated through the generations.

What I communicate to you here is nuanced. The Christian Establishment, by and large, perpetuates the notion that it is preferable to be a secret operative for Jesus, rather than externalize the entire Christian worldview. Besides regeneration being a gift beyond comprehension, it brings with it the simultaneous obligation to be obedient to Jesus in all areas of life and in all subject matters. There is no dichotomy between regeneration and its application. The humanist's worldview affects everything, over and against the Christian Establishment, whose worldview does not.

So often the Christian Establishment's obedience to our Lord calls for evangelizing that Jesus is the Savior and that obedience to our Lord means that we are to go and tell others how Jesus is the Savior. With that approach they have obeyed Jesus as Lord, but only by telling others about Jesus as Savior.

So often the Christian Establishment's obedience to our Lord calls for obeying Jesus in the New Testament, but not Jehovah in the Old Testament. After regeneration there tends to be a de-emphasis on matters that go beyond personal morality and into societal norms and civil law. Indeed, American Christendom encourages a newly regenerated Christian to act like Jesus in personal morality; in that respect, sending a child into a civil government school is ideal, as that is theoretically what Jesus *would* do. But Jesus would *not* get involved with societal norms, and most certainly not civil law—thus not civil government school system abolition. Sometimes this explains why children may be vessels in civil government schools for Jesus the Savior even though they do not understand the Christian worldview: *They do not need to understand the Christian worldview, except that Jesus is the Savior* and that He would have gone into a civil government school to save.

Stripped of His lordship and demoted to mere Savior, disobedience to Jesus as Lord over all is the reason the Christian teacher claims a clear conscience when going into a civil government school to be salt and light: his idea is to merely tell others about Jesus as Savior but not as Lord. The civil government school affords him that cover.

Above, I wrote that the Christian Establishment preacher is analogous to the out-of-touch Republican Establishment. The preacher has no understanding how the butcher, the baker, and the public policy maker operate in the real world, only he calls it *theology* instead of *theory*. Does the Christian Establishment have an answer as to how each is to externalize obedience to Jesus as Lord? Is each supposed to only tell people that Jesus saves, but not externalize Jesus' lordship in his respective calling? Sure, the Establishment has an answer when it comes to personal morality. But what about societal norms: contracts and covenants and keeping the shop clean? What about torts, surety, and mortgages? What about baking a cake for a homosexual wedding? What about ethics and honest weight and measures? These are not just civil law issues, since the Bible speaks to whether they are civil law issues in the first place. But where is the Christian Establishment's analysis for these people? Beyond personal morality the Christian Establishment has no answers.

Instead, the Christian Establishment operates under this unbiblical paradigm: a person is regenerated, and in conformity with how Jesus' lordship compels us to tell others that Jesus is the Savior and Lord, he tells a thousand others that Jesus is Savior and Lord. But at no point are those newly regenerated persons exposed to how we are to be obedient to Jesus the Lord in other ways, besides telling people that Jesus is the Savior and Lord! It is for that very reason that some Christians are charged with antinomianism.[122] Because theoretically you could have one million people regenerated, but they never externalize Jesus as Lord, except to tell others that He is Savior and Lord. Do you see? Suppose the butcher, the baker, and the public policy maker are all regenerated; then how, in each situation, does each externalize

---

[122] Meaning someone who is against a use for the law.

obedience to Jesus as Lord in societal norms and civil law? Bluntly put, the Christian Establishment says they do not need to.

The Christian Establishment has zero interest in extending Jesus' lordship over societal norms and they *certainly* have zero interest in extending Jesus' lordship over civil government. But when the public policy maker shows up to work he asks, *What should public policy be?* In response he is supposed to look to Scripture. In essence he is looking in Scripture for the answer to, *What is a justifiable use of the physical sword?* It is not discipling children. The Christian Establishment, in relying on humanism, thinks that Christians involved with civil government want to force others to do things. It is the exact opposite though, as we know that when Christians are involved with civil government, the civil government is to get smaller as the family and church governments get bigger. Social Security, Medicare, Medicaid, Obamacare, and other wealth transfer mechanisms are eliminated, in favor of private covenants and transactions. Moreover, civil government schools get smaller and are phased out through an increase in private education through family and church government obedience.

When I worked for the nation's largest auto insurance company, I was responsible for applying the standard auto policy. Under *Collision* coverage losses were covered that involved the policyholder's car in the event it struck another car or a person. Most people also had *Comprehensive* coverage, which would basically cover most (but not all) losses that were not covered by Collision coverage; Comprehensive coverage provided coverage in the event the car struck an animal. Anyway, one time a policyholder made the assertion that since he struck a human being it should be covered under Comprehensive; he made the assertion because he had Comprehensive coverage but not Collision coverage. Thus, he was trying to get the insurance company to accept his definition of *animal* to include *human*. Thankfully, for Christianity's sake, it did not work.

That story emphasizes how someone's worldview prevails with societal norms; someone's worldview prevails with civil law. Jesus' lordship does not end with personal morality. The Great Commission must not be segregated from societal norms and civil law. That is why it does not require the newly regenerated civil magistrate to resign, *after we have prayed for him to be regenerated.*[123] Jesus' lordship means that wherever one is, as best he can, he should deliver the gospel message of Jesus as Savior and Lord over all life's areas: limited health care for children, homelessness, poverty, the Iraq war, white-collar crime, human trafficking, global AIDS crisis, rampant fatherlessness, the greed behind the sub-prime mortgage crisis, the treatment of illegal aliens, and the plight of Christians just coming out of prison. *It is not enough though that the Christian merely works in these fields and*

---

[123] 1 Timothy 2:1-15.

shares the gospel when he comes across a non-Christian. The Christian must make the field itself reflect biblical principles, and show the non-Christian how that is the case.

The Christian worldview is coterminous with all of Scripture, not just with what Jesus did, to the exclusion of the Old Testament and Christianity, externalized in societal norms and civil law. A reasonable reading of John 1 means that all things were made through and for Jesus. Most things Jesus was not expressly involved in while on Earth; that does not mean we are not to extend obedience to Jesus into those areas. Jesus, as far as I can tell, was never a garbage man, chief financial officer, meter maid, fracking engineer, homemaker, SCUBA instructor, and so on. Does that mean we are not to extend obedience to Jesus into those professions? Of course not. The garbage man clears debris so society can be kept clean; the chief financial officer obeys biblical employer principles and economic and finance principles; the fracking engineer utilizes God's uniformity of nature to extract energy so missionaries can carry on the gospel; the homemaker teaches children and keeps the house in order; the SCUBA instructor facilitates exploring God's underwater creations. The reason obedience to Jesus extends into all those areas and professions is that there are then opportunities to apply God's principles (sanctification) so that people can be saved (salvation).

Externalizing obedience to Jesus as Lord matters to the abolition issue because if we are only to mimic Jesus, and resemble only His personal morality and maybe societal norms, but not civil law, then that obviously means that the preacher will not address whether the civil government schools should even exist.

The civil government's purpose is to glorify God; the only way that can happen is if the civil government is comprised of Christians. Yet the Christian Establishment believes Christians leading civil government are anathema. The Christian Establishment loathes Christian leadership, as they think it is advancing Christianity via the sword. The idea that Christians are to be society's leaders is, I think, generally accepted by American Christendom. But the Christian Establishment cut them down. Many Christians, thankfully, understand that Christian *lordship* is just Christian *leadership*. Through Christian leadership biblical law rises in visibility and then leads sinners to Christ. Those exercising Christian lordship in all areas of life are the ones honestly asking, *What would Jesus do?*

For years American Vision, including Gary North and Gary DeMar, has led the way in exploring the nuts and bolts of Christian leadership. I have benefited tremendously from their work, and I am thankful for them at least attempting to help other Christians with Christian leadership. Their theology is not theory; nor is it abstract and out of touch with reality. This idea of Jesus' lordship in all areas of life is often called *Dominion*.[124] But John Piper says, "The closer we get to Dominion Theology, the closer we get to living by the sword."[125] But this indicts the Christian Establishment, for they are the ones who think it is perfectly acceptable for Christians to use the physical sword to proselytize in civil government schools. The dominionist thinks the civil government is only for promoting good and punishing evildoers; the dominionist holds that the Bible does not justify a civil government school's existence. Piper himself adamantly declares, "We never, ever, ever undertake with the sword to advance the gospel. Ever!"[126] Really? Has Piper ever condemned the civil government school system's existence?

Christian lordship, through societal norms and civil law, calls for Christian leadership *over others*. Societal norms require Christians to frame reality— to assert a human is not an animal; and civil laws require Christians to frame reality—to properly articulate good and evil. Societal norms and civil

---

[124] As per Genesis 1:26: "Let us make man in our image, after our likeness. And let them have dominion over the fish of the sea and over the birds of the heavens and over the livestock and over all the earth and over every creeping thing that creeps on the earth."

[125] "Dominion Theology of Reconstructionism" (Desiring God, 1 April 1994, Web. 25, March 2016).

[126] John Piper, "Subjection to God and Subjection to Man" (Video http://www.desiringgod.org/messages/subjection-to-god-and-subjection-to-the-state-part-4. March 25, 2016.

law inform people about what is proper and hopefully expose a person's sin and need for a Savior. Each Christian Establishment member should realize that proper Christian lordship would make the civil government school system smaller and the church government congregations larger!

Through disobedience to our Lord Jesus, the Christian Establishment disengages the humanist's church, the civil government school system, negatively affecting the gospel. *And the gospel, my friends, is of supreme importance.*

Near where I sometimes walk there is spray-painted graffiti on an abandoned building that reads, "Those who criticize our generation forget who raised it." The Christian Establishment should see it. The Christian Establishment, after every immoral Supreme Court decision, convenes to ask, "How do we better engage society?" Then, for posturing purposes, they issue a press release saying they have devised a strategy. The problem is the strategy never includes questioning whether there should be civil government schools. *The Christian Establishment wants to engage the very society they themselves raised.*

It is the case that whatever reality we introduce to our children is obviously going to be their starting point in life. This partially explains the development of immorality in our society relative to marriage. Decades ago no-fault divorce became societally normal, and was then eventually codified by civil law; that morphed into other forms of acceptable societal norms and then civil laws codifying pornography and homosexuality. While there are other factors affecting one's perception of reality, his starting point, as introduced to him by the existing generations, cannot be discounted. As societal norms and civil law informed us that no-fault divorce, pornography, and homosexuality are

181

acceptable, that took us further and further into humanistic territory.

The way this plays out in society is, while heartbreaking, quite simple. You go to church on Sunday, and it is most likely the case that you never hear about civil government limits. It could be because your preacher misunderstands Romans 13, or he misunderstands Christian freedom, or he thinks Jesus is coming back soon, or he does not believe we are to be obedient to Jesus in all areas of life. Along with that, the Sunday service, mail solicitations, emails, radio shows, Sunday and Wednesday church classes, and every other Christian medium that comes your way never articulates civil government limits, so it has never occurred to you that there should not be civil government schools. Because you (and pretty much every other person you know) have never pondered whether civil government schools should exist, the system continues. The system's victims grow up and implement the humanism they were taught. The humanism informs the next generation, including Christians.

In terms of introducing reality to subsequent generations, I have mentioned Social Security, Medicare, Medicaid, and so on. Have you ever questioned those things? Probably not, as you were never taught to question them, especially not in the civil government schools. Separate from the issue as to whether you could muster the political will to abolish socialistic programs, you were likely never prompted to get to the threshold issue of even questioning those things.

Sometimes the Christian Establishment asserts that if the Christians would have done their job in the first place (helped the poor, tended the ill, and so on), there never would have been the need for civil government taking over those duties that belong to private citizens. But that is something they cannot, at least to my satisfaction, know and prove. They cannot prove it was the church failing that caused the civil government to intrude on the church's jurisdiction. Moreover, *it is irrelevant*, because even if the church fails, it does not justify the civil government venturing into territory where they have no authority. So even if it is conceded that the church failed to help the poor and tend the ill, the proper civil government action would have been to do *nothing*. That may sound harsh, but the bigger danger is that, when the civil government goes outside their jurisdiction, bad things happen; they make things worse. God designed reality that way.

Introducing subsequent generations to a Christian reality is necessary to advance the gospel. But when children are first introduced to a humanistic reality, gospel evangelism becomes more difficult. I can hear it now as the predictable Christian Establishment preacher claims the Holy Ghost has never encountered the impenetrable heart. I agree with that. But at the same time I know of no Christian who discounts human strategy in evangelism.

When a child spends thirteen years groomed in a system that excludes Jesus and fills the vacuum with humanistic principles, that child's conscience is seared. The civil government school system is a thirteen-year system that precludes Jesus being the rationale for all wisdom; it is a thirteen-year system that promotes each man be a law unto himself; it is a thirteen-year system that teaches how man is the measure of all things; it is a thirteen-year system that emphasizes man is the ultimate authority. *So why is the Christian Establishment surprised that young people are abandoning the Christian worldview?* They have been told for thirteen years that Christianity is not true. Their consciences are seared more and more every day by the civil government school system. Yet the Christian Establishment does nothing about it.

Failing to introduce subsequent generations to a Christian reality is to the gospel's peril. When young people are exposed to the gospel and the out workings of a fully extended lordship through a Christian education, they may not be immediately regenerated but at least they have heard the gospel presentation, and it is then the humanist's burden to overcome (including with work by expending resources). On the contrary, a civil government school system delays a person's exposure to the gospel, and then subsequent sanctification. Then Christians are stuck expending resources on not just teaching Christianity but undoing humanism. Why not just teach Christianity in the first place?

Besides, we never know when a person will remember the gospel presentation he or she heard in a Christian educational environment. With education centered on Jesus, we have *at least* most people subscribing to God-fearingness and some being born again. As it stands now, with an education system centered on man, we have *at best* most people subscribing to suppressing the truth in unrighteousness and some with outright conscience-searing.

The unchallenged assumption that the civil government school system is proper has penetrated every area of society and is not easily undone. As Bruce Shortt so thoroughly and impressively demonstrated in his book *The Harsh Truth About Public Schools*, many organizations, entities, and paradigms rely on the money flowing from the civil government, thus "efforts to restore a focus on traditional educational and moral values cannot succeed because the necessary changes would threaten too many powerful constituencies. Moreover, any change that would imperil the flow of dollars to schools and their spending constituencies will meet determined opposition."[127] While civil government schools cannot be reformed (as they should not exist in the first place, even if Christian) Shortt's point remains intact; civil government schools are entrenched in our society, so much so that they have tainted the pulpit's condemnation of them.

---

[127] Bruce N. Shortt, *The Harsh Truth About Public Schools*, (Vallecito, California: Chalcedon, 2004), 244.

Our society has this existing paradigm, and since the Christian Establishment never questions it, American Christendom never questions it, so subsequent generations never question it. The civil government school system's existence is so entrenched in our society that nobody ever questions it. Thus, unless someone like me comes along to question it, outside the Christian Establishment's purview, generationally nothing changes. In fact, things get incrementally worse, because young people are not only *not* taught by their Christian parents that the civil government has limits, but humanists continually expand the civil government to the family and church government's detriment. The civil government school was developed to do the very business of making the family and church governments smaller. Anyone who is *willing* to see that *can* see that.

For purposeful reiteration, Scripture informs us there are multiple governments: family, church, and civil. The Christian Establishment never addresses how each is limited, and for a variety of reasons, never questions the civil government school system's existence. So it continues as a generational mechanism that perpetuates an anti-Christian perspective of life and reality. That anti-Christian perspective is disobedience to God, which brings down God's curses on us. Because we continue to incur God's curses, the gospel is negatively affected. It is for the gospel's sake in Deuteronomy 6:4-9 that God commands fathers:

Hear, O Israel: The LORD our God, the LORD is one. You shall love the LORD your God with all your heart and with all your soul and with all your might. And these words that I command you today shall be on your heart. You shall teach them diligently to your children, and shall talk of them when you sit in your house, and when you walk by the way, and when you lie down, and when you rise. You shall bind them as a sign on your hand, and they shall be as frontlets between your eyes. You shall write them on the doorposts of your house and on your gates.

Later in Deuteronomy 6 there are verses 20-25:

When your son asks you in time to come, "What is the meaning of the testimonies and the statutes and the rules that the Lord our God has commanded you?" then you shall say to your son, "We were Pharaoh's slaves in Egypt. And the Lord brought us out of Egypt with a mighty hand. And the Lord showed signs and wonders, great and grievous, against Egypt and against Pharaoh and all his household, before our eyes. And he brought us out from there, that he might bring us in and give us the land that he swore to give to our fathers. And the Lord commanded us to do all these statutes, to fear the Lord our God, for our good always, that he might preserve us alive, as we are this day. And it will be righteousness for us, if we are careful to do all this commandment before the Lord our God, as he has commanded us."

In the Deuteronomy passages no matter how you define "these words," "testimonies," "statutes," and "rules," you must admit there is a generational concept. So often these passages are unilaterally dismissed as inapplicable to the Church. But those who carelessly dismiss Deuteronomy 6 do not deal with the generational concept undergirding the whole chapter: God commands fathers to teach subsequent generations His principles. That means that even those people who disregard the Old Testament principles in favor of what is repeated in the New Testament, still have principles that must be perpetuated generationally.

Besides, I think it is responsible and accurate to say that Deuteronomy 6:4-9 has been republished in the New Testament: "You shall love the Lord your God with all your heart and with all your soul and with all your mind", we are told in Matthew 22:37. So two concepts undergird biblical education, one substantive and one procedural: that we are to love the Lord with all the heart, soul, and mind (substantive); and we are to teach our children that parents are supposed to teach that to their children (procedural).

Nevertheless, even if someone dismisses Deuteronomy 6:4-9 there is Ephesians 6:4: "Fathers, do not provoke your children to anger, but bring them up in the discipline and instruction of the Lord." Still further there is Psalms 145:3-4: "Great is the Lord, and greatly to be praised, and his greatness is unsearchable. One generation shall commend your works to another, and shall declare your mighty acts." And Psalms 78:5-8 commands generational teaching:

> He decreed statutes for Jacob and established the law in Israel, which he commanded our ancestors to teach their children, so the next generation would know them, even the children yet to be born, and they in turn would tell their children. Then they would put their trust in God and would not forget his deeds but would keep his commands. They would not be like their ancestors—a stubborn and rebellious generation, whose hearts were not loyal to God, whose spirits were not faithful to him.

And so does Psalms 48:12-14: "Walk about Zion, go around her, number her towers, consider well her ramparts, go through her citadels, that you may tell the next generation that this is God, our God forever and ever. He will guide us forever."

The blindingly obvious lesson that the Christian Establishment fails to address, and literally to our own peril, is that education produces society. (So when things get bad and the Christian Establishment wants to reassess how to engage society, they whiff, since they fail to deal with the civil government school system.) That is, education is not an ideological plank within a religious platform. **Education *is* the platform!** The humanists recognized this after Robert Owen's failed New Harmony communist colony. The late Samuel Blumenfeld preserves that fact for us in his *Is Public Education Necessary?* "The great lesson learned by Owen and his followers was that education had to precede the creation of a communist society, for the people educated under the old system were too selfish, too uncooperative, too incorrigible."[128]

Education drives society.[129] And despite American Christendom's best efforts to affirmatively educate

---

[128] Samuel L. Blumenfeld, *Is Public Education Necessary?,* (Powder Springs, GA: American Vision Press, 2011), 66.

[129] In a conversation to which I was not a party, Paul Weyrich (founder of the Christian Right and leading political strategist) said this: "[When] conservatives win elections the Left still wins because they control the culture. Culture always trumps politics. You're doing the right thing by helping families and

some children in the nurture and admonition of the Lord, there are still civil government schools. So, on the one hand, we have an increasingly *affirmative* awareness of private Christian education, but American Christendom (as long as there is no *negative* awareness against the civil government discipling the next generation) is a one-legged duck swimming in a circle.[130]

Oftentimes there is a false dichotomy drawn between encouraging private, Christian education on the one hand and my abolition position on the other. It is not my contention that we need one or the other; it is my contention that we need both; but we do not have the latter. It may be the case that we have some Christian organizations engaging society on education. Indeed, as a total percentage of American Christendom, this still seems to be a token percentage. Nevertheless, *no* frontline organization is engaging the humanist's church—the civil government school system. Those frontline organizations are the Christian Establishment.

It is not my contention that every organization must change their mission to abolition; but to the degree that they speak about education, they must

---

churches choose Christian or home schools." Culture (personal morality and societal norms) drives politics (public policy).

[130] See *The Promise of Jonadab: Building a Christian Family Legacy in a Time of Cultural Decline* by E. Ray Moore and Gail Pinckney Moore (Greenville, SC: Ambassador, 2010).

articulate the abolition end goal. In practice this means organizations that concentrate on Genesis 1:1, and to the degree they talk about education (which they do), they would do so within the biblical framework of private education, to the civil government's exclusion. In a complementary fashion I do the same: I focus on abolition, and to the degree I talk about Genesis 1:1, I do so within the biblical framework of the literal six-day Creation. But what if I said, "I am only going to focus on abolition and when it comes to Creation I will just say it is unimportant whether we evolved"? Would that not be ridiculous?

Likewise, this means pro-family organizations, which deal with public education policy, must change their statements from trying to (impossibly) harmonize the biblical, parental control model and the humanistic, local control model, to expressly state that the civil government has no business being in the education business.

It has been said that morality *cannot* be legislated; that it *can* be legislated has also been said. I find that the disagreement is a function of attaching different meanings to the saying. On the one hand, saying that morality cannot be legislated means that merely enacting a public policy will not force those subject to it to act in conformity. On the other hand, saying that morality can be legislated means that legislation is anchored to an ultimate authority. Both proponents talk past one another.

I find that both meanings are true. Producing legislation does not always cause the intended positive result; in fact, if the people do not want the law in the first place, the law is not likely to be enacted. That is no different than disregarding God's Law: one is going to rebel against that to which he does not want to submit. On the other hand, legislation is anchored to an ultimate authority—a society's god.[131] In merging both definitions of legislating morality, really what we have is civil law. It is civil law because it is public policy as a function of a society's collective ultimate authority that has behind it the physical sword—*legislating morality*.

Putting all this together, as it now stands we have legislating morality via civil government schools. Frighteningly, the civil government is discipling the generations, *forcing* their disciples to conform to what the civil government says they should conform to. It is subscribing to the opinion that man can reward and punish thought, that man in reliance on the physical sword can, in essence, coerce what to think.

Because the civil government now controls discipling the generations, those young people are taught humanism. They are taught that man is the measure of all things, the ultimate authority, and the lawgiver. Consequently, those young people grow

---

[131] Rousas J. Rushdoony and Herbert W. Titus, *The Institutes of Biblical Law: A Chalcedon Study*. (Nutley, NJ: Craig Press, 1973.

up to externalize humanism through their "church"; the civil government school is the local diocese. They are merely doing what they were taught for thirteen years at the local diocese. And if they themselves are not the civil government actor, coercing thought with the physical sword, they vote for others who are. That the civil government is in control of what our young people think and that the civil government is in control of discipling the nations is not a coincidence; they know what they are doing. They have exceeded their jurisdiction, against God's commands, and taken on the education duty. The Christian Establishment allows this.

The fact that civil government school disciples grow up and implement humanistic civil law is a detriment to the gospel. We are literally seeing this exact battle now (as I write this) between sodomy and marriage. Humanistic civil law is hostile to the gospel, doing its best to be a speed bump or outright roadblock to what is head-on with humanism: Christianity. God's church is attacked: our right to speak about homosexuality (and, therefore, repentance and grace) is inhibited; the church's nonprofit status is attacked (which negatively affects resources that contribute to the spread of the gospel); and so on. *But still the Christian Establishment refuses to address the civil government school system's existence.*

When civil law is humanistic it causes curses on society, which negatively affect the gospel. Higher taxes are curses; they drain resources from Bible production. Increased civil government regulations are curses; they cause the pulpit to stay far away from civil government and public policy analysis. Public policies protecting sexual immorality are curses; they make the biblical definition of marriage hate speech and lessen the father's education responsibility. International trade becomes the business of the "neutral" civil government bureaucrat; he displaces the evangelistic overseas business man. History is republished by the civil government, as the new victor in the battle of past interpretation, and that same history is emptied of its Christian content. Economics and finance are reframed in a way that moves a society towards adopting the perspective that private property and, therefore, private wealth are hostile to achieving a humanistic utopian dream.[132] And, of course, all these planks are taught in the civil government schools—ground zero for perpetuating humanism. The gospel gets harder to perpetuate, as society expunges not just the money from the Christian's pocketbook, but his voice from the public square. The examples are indefinite, showing how, if we do not obey God's commands, there will be repercussions. Those repercussions – or curses – negatively affect the gospel.

The Christian Establishment's civil government school system disengagement negatively affects the

---

[132] It is the humanist, or the Christian who thinks like one, who believes in salvation by legislation. The Christian Establishment thinks like humanists.

gospel. The civil government disciples grow up and externalize humanistic societal norms and civil law. Christianity is pushed out of the public sphere and marginalized, giving the impression it is not a bona fide belief system.[133] Thereafter it becomes harder, even in minor ways, to spread the gospel. There is nothing worse than hitting the Christian Establishment with the harsh truth that the Great Commission is abdicated. I can say very few things with stronger emphasis than education *is* the Great Commission. Because the Christian Establishment guts the Great Commission through Romans 13 negligence, end-times speculation, Christian freedom, or disobedience to Jesus' lordship, the Great Commission is truncated, striated, compartmentalized. The Christian Establishment hates, for good reason, top down Christianity. But if they hated top down humanism half as much, we would not be in the mess we are in now, as the gospel is suffering tremendously because of humanistic civil government impeding the gospel.

Despite our (deserved) curses, the Christian Establishment still refuses to engage what is causing it all. Because of Romans 13 negligence, they never question whether the civil government has limits; thus the civil government school is never

---

[133] It is, in fact, the case that the Christian worldview facilitates its own rejection. Cornelius Van Til, the great apologist, showed how non-Christians can only reject Christianity *because* Christianity is true. For example, for the non-Christian to rely on logic to refute Christianity is in itself a reliance on Christianity, for logic emanates from Christianity.

questioned. Consequently, millions of young people are taught a gospel that is no gospel at all. They grow up to further perpetuate the paradigm, causing a further hindrance of the Christian worldview. Because of end-times speculation, the Christian Establishment forbears externalizing Christian societal norms and civil law; therefore, civil government schools are never abolished. Consequently, millions of young people are taught a gospel that is no gospel at all. They grow up to further perpetuate the paradigm, causing a further hindrance of the Christian worldview. Because of Christian freedom, the Christian Establishment erroneously frames the issue as one of delegation and not jurisdiction; consequently, civil government schools march on. Consequently, millions of young people are taught a gospel that is no gospel at all. They grow up to further perpetuate the paradigm, causing a further hindrance of the Christian worldview. And because of disobedience to Jesus' lordship, the Christian Establishment effectuates Jesus' mere salvific capabilities; as a result, Jesus is never exalted to be Lord over thought. Consequently, millions of young people are taught a gospel that is no gospel at all. They grow up to further perpetuate the paradigm, causing a further hindrance of the Christian worldview.

Oftentimes at a seminar, home school convention, or conference I am told, "You will never abolish civil government schools." I respond, "We are already doing it." I live for that response.

In explaining the jurisdiction issue I am consistently asked about the single mother of four who relies on a civil government school. The implication is that I am proposing something awful in abolition, as it would allegedly remove the single mother's only viable option in educating her children. As is often the case the questioner exposes his worldview when asking that question. Thus, what the questioner is really suggesting is that the civil government school's existence is a problem solver and not a problem creator. In that regard it was supposedly the civil government that came to the single mother's rescue, not Christians. The questioner exposes how little faith he has in Christianity being a problem solver. And it is not the Christian who would be responsible for any consequences incurred during the transition to abolition; it is the humanist. God will bless us during that time, not curse us.

If the Christian Establishment thinks public policy does not matter, each should come down from his high place and go where the people are: where real life takes place, where theology is not an abstraction but something that affects lives.[134] Piper's limited health care for children, homelessness, poverty, and so on are only positively affected by the gospel when principles (*when propositional truths from Scripture*) are presented to Christians on such matters. Principles from Scripture solve society's problems. But more than that, the propositional truths in Scripture do not justify civil government schools, so, upon abolition, limited health care for children, homelessness, and poverty can all be prevented to a greater degree, as young people would be taught the worldview that has the answers to society's problems.

If anyone in the Christian Establishment holds that Jesus did not come to get involved with public policy, I want to see him get face to face with a man who makes ten dollars an hour and whose landlord's property taxes just went up; I want to see him visit his state's department of education, and observe the costly and unnecessary complexity, and how that money could be returned to his congregation; I want him to see how a state's union policies force Christians to pay for humanistic lobbying. I want him, instead of just espousing abstract theology, to understand that *theology affects public policy*, and public policy affects how

---

[134] Luther justifiably scolded Erasmus for asserting that the debate between freewill and predestination was an irrelevant abstract. How much more relevant than that debate is the one over jurisdiction over your child's thoughts? Luther, Martin, J I. Packer, and O R. Johnston. *The Bondage of the Will*. Grand Rapids: Baker Academic, 1957. 44.

people live, and how people live affects whether the gospel is perpetuated—so whether someone spends eighty trillion years or more with God.

I would like to see the Christian Establishment preacher go in front of an inner city congregation comprised of black people. Can it honestly be said that public policy does not affect those people? Has no-fault divorce negatively affected a father's requirement to stay with his wife and, therefore, his children—and then subsequently teach his children about Jesus? Do property taxes not disproportionately injure low income people and, therefore, preclude their homeschooling opportunities? Does the fact that the civil government is getting larger and larger not take jobs away from men who otherwise would be providing for their families? These things matter. Public policy affects lives. The Christian Establishment never takes the time to understand this; they think what I endorse is using the sword to spread Christianity.

While it may be the case that some in the Christian Establishment do deal with public policy, they are part of the problem, since they do not deal with abolition. Once again, they deal with the symptoms the civil government school produces and not the disease. That was the Moral Majority's problem. *It was not the case that the Moral Majority failed because they became involved with politics; they failed because, while they affected public policy, they did not simultaneously deal with the source of the humanistic public policy they were up against.* God bless the Moral Majority, but if they promoted abolition in the late 1970s and early 1980s, America's trajectory would have been altogether different. We would have eventually been able to scale back the political efforts and merely cultivate America's Christian education environment. Public policy is fruit: we must eliminate the humanist's rotting tree, root and all.

Despite the Christian Establishment's misunderstanding of government, policy does not start with *civil* government. That means it is the family government and church government as the starting point to policy. But here is the nuance you must understand: it is not the case that I am agreeing with the Christian Establishment when it comes to education starting at home. The disagreement I have with the Christian Establishment is that I believe education should include educating young people how there should not be civil government schools; the Christian Establishment disregards that. That is why, generationally, we are on a downward spiral. We are experiencing the opposite of a revival.

Policy starts with family government and church government. Family government policy should be private education; proper Christian education policy does not include force and coercion. In conjunction with how family government education should be private and, of course, Christ-centered, the church government should preach those truths. So while the family government *teaches* all subjects via Jesus, the church government *preaches* all subjects via Jesus. (Do you see how this is supposed to work?) Then, when the children who are educated with the true biblical knowledge that force and coercion have no place in advancing Christ-centeredness, they grow up to be our next public policymakers. Then, as civil government actors and voters, they work towards abolition. With the Christian Establishment, though, because there is never preaching that there should not be civil government schools, they facilitate leaving intact the civil government schools' infrastructure.

The churches are to reinforce all this; in fact, it cannot necessarily be expected that people new to the church even realize that God gave original jurisdiction to the families when it comes to discipling. It is from the pews they should hear this truth. Currently, anecdotally but confidently, I wager that in less than one percent of our churches does the family assume original jurisdiction over education. This is where the Christian Establishment preacher relies on generational teaching: his congregation is likely comprised of civil government school stakeholders. He defers to their model instead of God's.

The two main tyrannical components to civil government schools are compulsory education and taxes. Those are addressed above. Here, I tell you that any movement on public policy can be incremental, but it must move in the proper direction. In a conversation I once had with a home school family, I was told that conservatives are unlike humanists in that we do not accept incremental victories, and, thus, we do not achieve our goals. As evidence of this, education vouchers were cited. I countered that education vouchers are not conservative public policy; rather, they are humanistic public policy. They rely on compulsory taxation, the proceeds of which go to a gatekeeper, who then requires certain parameters be met in order for the voucher to be useable. That is not Christianity; it is humanism.

The humanist favors education vouchers, as they are socialistic central planning with humanist gatekeepers, inextricable with physical power via civil government, the vehicle by which the humanist asserts man's ultimate authority. Education vouchers allow humanists to continue manipulating others, including children. A true education voucher system is this and the only voucher system I support: you keep your money and I keep mine; you educate your children and I educate mine. If you need help tell me, and we can help one another without financial gatekeepers and school boards. School boards are for Russians, not Americans. All that is to say that incrementalism is okay; just make sure you are working for the proper goal, and that is to abolish civil government schools.

Compulsory education is a crime against God and it is the most direct attack on His sovereignty that I can think of. Every state in the union has compulsory education laws. If you inspect each state's compulsory education verbiage, most say something like, "Attendance required between these ages, except in these enumerated circumstances." When they say "attendance required" they mean attendance at a civil government school. Thus, the default is that your child must attend a civil government school. To opt your child out of civil government school attendance you must prove to the civil government that your situation falls within the statute. That could include how your child attends a private school, as defined by the civil government. That could mean how your child is home schooled by someone certified, as defined by the civil government. But no matter how you slice it, you have to spend time convincing the civil government that what you are doing is "legal."

There are numerous problems with compulsory school attendance laws. First, the civil government does not have the right to force you to do something, like attend a civil government school. Second, the laws treat someone not in conformity as a criminal. This is harassment in disguise. Third, the burden should not fall on the parent to convince the civil government he is qualified to teach. Rather, the burden should be on the civil government that a parent committed some evil act. Finally, the civil government has no right to force you to associate with others.

Compulsory education laws obviously must be eliminated. Incrementally this means making the age window smaller. If your state civil government requires attendance starting at age five, then change it to six; if your state civil government requires civil government school attendance until age eighteen, then change it to seventeen.

Not incidentally, I am asked quite often how millions of children would be educated if there were no civil government schools. Oftentimes the inquiry is phrased in such a way that implies that millions of children must be educated *en masse*. What I try to avoid is adopting the inquirer's assumptions. First, I do not assume that millions of children are currently "educated" in civil government schools. Why do I not assume that? Because education without Jesus as the rationale is not only futile, it is impossible. If you are a Christian you must know that you cannot know something without God allowing you to know it. That's Revelation. And so-called education without Jesus as the rationale (which is a civil government school's legally required model) is one big giant truth suppression machine. Besides that, statistics abound showing how unintelligent young people are after thirteen years of hard time in a civil government school.

Second, I don't assume that civil government schools are the solution to anything. It is not a hypothetical that children are being lost to confusion every day. Dropout rates have been estimated to be as high as 7,000 students per school day.[135] What the questioner does for those children now is the answer to what he would do for those children if there were no civil government schools. So the answer falls on the questioner, not me.

Finally, I don't assume *millions* of children need to be educated. *Only one child at a time needs to be educated.* Do you see? Humanists try to get you to assume that the only entity that can handle millions of students is the civil government. But millions of students do not need to be educated. That is because families do not have millions of children. They have one, or two, or three, or ten. But any of those numbers is significantly less than "millions." Christians often justify the civil government school system in that they hold that only the civil government is large enough to "educate" our children. But that is begging the question: the civil government is only large because they *are* operating schools, not because they *should* be.

Once civil government schools are abolished, the student pupil ratio will improve. God knows what He is doing; He created a biblical model that is best for children: mom and dad, teaching the Christian worldview, always. When a humanist (or a Christian who thinks like one) presents a common

---

[135] "11 Facts About High School Dropout Rates," *Do Something*, https://www.dosomething.org/us/facts/11-facts-about-high-school-dropout-rates, (March 26, 2016. I do not think the number can be that high, but if it is, praise Jesus. Children ought to run out of civil government schools just as if the building itself were on fire.

argument like what I just dissected, use the Christian worldview to crush that humanistic thinking. It is rubbish and cannot stand against our Creator's eternal and infinite wisdom. For your child's benefit adopt God's education model.

Regarding taxes that support civil government schools, there should not be any. Socialism is biblically improper in that the civil government has the right to tax for only those biblical ends for which they have authority: promoting good and punishing evildoers. So an unbiblical end shall have no underlying claim on taxes to support that end. No tax, whether levied on personal or real property, shall be used for operating civil government schools. Thus, those taxes must be eliminated, even if only incrementally.

The real property[136] tax, like compulsory education, is repugnant to the Christian worldview because it makes by default man (via the civil government) the landowner, and if one does not pay his perpetually levied tax, then man (via the civil government) steals his property.[137] In other words, it is the humanist and the Christian Establishment that perpetuates the lie that we steward the land to man. We steward the land to God; public policy must reflect that truth, and all real property taxes must be

---

[136] *Real property* is land and anything permanently attached to it.
[137] Sometimes it is claimed that mortgages are as evil, but those are voluntary agreements. Real property taxes are not voluntary.

eliminated. That would fatally wound the civil government's system.

Christians oftentimes buy into the humanistic wealth-sharing ideology, as if the pragmatic way to educate our children is through taxation. But while sharing is a Christian concept, the apostles did it[138] outside force and coercion. "Sharing" through paying your taxes is not sharing. Anyone who believes in civil government wealth "sharing" mechanisms is a socialist and operating under the humanism banner.

An important sidebar to the taxation issue is that humanists are fond of using poor people and children as justification for humanism. In many states, including Virginia (where I live), gambling and lotteries are legal. And some of those revenues are channeled to civil government schools, so there is the assertion that children benefit from those sins.[139] Low-income people, though, are more likely to gamble and play lotteries; indeed, then, new schools are built quite frequently with taxpayer funds that, for the most part, came from low-income individuals. So money is taken disproportionately from low-income people to be transferred to central planners, so that they can help poor people! Ridiculous. All civil government school-funding mechanisms must be severed from the civil government schools.

---

[138] Acts 4.

[139] They are sins because they facilitate faith in randomness and luck and not God's Providence.

We must eliminate humanistic entities that hinder the gospel. This includes the federal civil government's Department of Education, all state civil government departments of education, and all regional organizations, such as the Southern Regional Education Board and the Interstate Compact on Educational Opportunities for Military. Local humanistic entities, like the Southwest Virginia Consortium on Education, and all local civil government school boards also must be abolished.

Enacting public policy is, of course, the eventual goal. But there must first exist the political will for that public policy to be enacted. In that regard the biggest weapon (besides actual public policy implementation) is *debating* whether there should be civil government schools. This gets us half way there. For example, when the sodomy movement was given the ability to engage Christians, they won ground. With the mere engagement of the opposition and the mere acknowledgement of the sodomy movement, there was something bona fide and legitimate to be against. And for those humanists and "Christians" who never thought about sodomy, they were easily persuaded. Thus, by merely getting a public debate with American Christendom on how there should not be civil government schools, we will gain converts. Even if just a few, it was more than before.

When I say we can win converts by getting a public debate on the civil government schools issue, this does *not* mean that we should be debating delegation—whether to delegate one's education duty to the civil government. That is, in fact, the problem: the Christian Establishment is "debating" the wrong thing.[140] It matters what is debated, because something debated contains underlying principles, and therefore underlying assumptions. For example, the Christian Establishment has indoctrinated American Christendom to rhetorically ask, "What about the single mother who cannot afford to privately educate her child?" The better question to ask is, "Why is my church not preaching how the civil government is impeding that single mother's right to privately educate her child?" Or, "Why is my church not fighting tooth and nail to get back the jurisdiction lost to them, so that they can help that single mother?" The Christian Establishment, because they have American Christendom's eyes and ears, can short circuit an America ready for abolition by merely questioning the civil government school system's existence.

If you are not already aware, the Christian Establishment does not like to tread new territory. They feel safe with telling everybody that Jesus is the Messiah and that we are to tell others that fact. They do not want to venture into societal norms and civil law, because that could cause disagreement.

---

[140] I quote "debating" because, for the most part, there is no debate on the issue, on the claim it is divisive.

They feel safe equating evangelism with being nice. This is exactly why some denominations tend to have larger congregations, as there is nothing on which to disagree: there is no discussion and debate on whether the civil government can tax for and build roads, or on whether the Bible requires a father to earn a paycheck, or on whether the death penalty is binding on the sexually immoral. There is a discussion and debate vacuum relative to societal norms and civil law, and so there is less divisiveness. Less divisiveness means bigger congregations. Is the Christian Establishment preacher ready to trade truth for less tithing? Is the Christian Establishment pro-family organization ready to trade truth for a smaller donor base? Is the Christian Establishment attorney ready to trade truth for pro bono work?

I enjoy how humanistic leaders externalize their worldview. I hate humanism, but I love the brashness and matter-of-factness the humanist leader has. Starting companies, defining reality, challenging paradigms—marriage, economics. Christians, by and large, do none of that. American Christendom has very few answers for humanism because the Christian Establishment has led us to believe the gospel is impotent. For some reason the Christian Establishment is comfortable defining Jesus as a person worth emulating, even though we can never be exactly like Jesus, but they are loathe to propound the goal of civil government school system abolition, even if (they think) we can never

212

get there; they do not want to even define the goal we are supposedly sure to fall short of.

Narrowing compulsory education age windows and eliminating property taxes are top priorities. But walking right out of a civil government school's front door eventually takes funds from that school.[141] Walking right out the front door was Robert Browne's basic idea in his *Reformation Without Tarrying for Anie*.[142] Robert Browne was a Separatist. Amid the debate about "reforming" the civil government's control over the Church of England, Robert Browne realized there was no need to unnecessarily submit to the civil government as the gatekeeper.[143] To be sure, he properly understood that the civil government did not have control over doctrine, and any attempts to "reform" the Church of England was conceding a false premise in that the civil government had any say in the matter in the first place. Thus, he seceded from the Church of England, and he had no gatekeeper stopping him from espousing the truth. To put what Browne did in contemporary terms, he realized we do not need the civil government's permission to say that there should not be a civil government school system; we can walk right out the front door and preach that truth.

---

[141] This does not mean that the funds would immediately go back into your pocket.

[142] Robert Browne, *Reformation Without Tarrying for Anie* (Boston: Directors of the Old South Work, 1899).

[143] With full disclosure in mind Browne eventually went back to the Church of England.

Robert Browne understood jurisdiction, thus he knew that something that should not exist cannot be reformed. He knew a church under the civil government's control could not be reformed, as that church should not exist in the first instance. It was harder for Browne to make that decision;[144] here and now we will still have the freedom to reject the civil government school system.

I rely on Browne's example for two reasons. First, that a civil government school cannot be reformed, as it should not exist in the first place. Even if it were overtly Christian it would still be an unbiblical institution. And second, as I stated above, private education and abolition are two sides of the same coin. When private education increases it simultaneously increases the political will for abolition: parents have their children back, then they build a caucus of political will moving towards recovering their tax dollars. The bottom line is that, for a child to have a Christian education in the United States, the child can walk right out the front door and get one. There is literally nothing (absent being "qualified" through the civil government gatekeeper) stopping you from teaching your child the Christian worldview.

Many Christian Establishment attorneys waste money on litigating the supposed right to publicly pray in civil government schools or give a Christian

---

[144] He had to move to another country to propound separatist doctrine.

speech at a graduation ceremony, and so on. But we already have the right to do those things: in non-civil government schools; there is no need to sue for them. You see, to sue somebody for the supposed right to publicly pray in Jesus' name in a civil government school is conceding the false premise that there should be civil government schools.[145] Christians already have the right to pray publicly in Jesus' name, and the Free Exercise Clause protects this. Thus, like Robert Browne, by leveraging the freedoms we already have, we need not unnecessarily petition gatekeepers who are operating under an unbiblical paradigm. The Church of England was operating under an unbiblical paradigm; so is the civil government school system. Policy does not always need to pass through the civil government. You can "implement" proper policy by relying on the freedoms we already have (private education options) to teach the next generation that the civil government has no right to operate schools. Over the years that policy will be implemented, all via the path of least resistance, and by relying exactly on the very thing on which we should always rely: the spiritual sword.

---

[145] Oftentimes in these lawsuits attorney fees are awarded if the Christian wins. But to the degree possible, the Christian attorney's resources would be better allocated to a private school or home school group. That mitigates, over the long term, the judge being a gatekeeper to Christianity. Eventually the private school or home school student could grow up and replace the humanist judge and hopefully make legal decisions based on biblical law.

The key to abolition is dealing with the funding mechanisms. And the basic rule of thumb is that you want to keep your money in the first place. So vouchers and tax credits are a non-starter. Education savings accounts seem productive, but the problem there is that the civil government still regulates our money and they still have our tax dollars. So while savings accounts may be good investment vehicles, they do not deal with getting our money back.

Understand that on the local level it is worth the time to fight bond issues and tax increases that are proposed for civil government schools. That is because if the bonds are issued or the taxes increased, it directly damages the private education community. They have to pay more even though they do not use the civil government school system. Each local civil government generally must have a balanced budget, so if money can be taken from the civil government schools, it can then be utilized right away to advance the gospel.

Regarding policy generally, our money needs to be allocated towards teaching Christianity in the first instance instead of unteaching humanism after thirteen years in a civil government school system. It is for that reason I stopped giving to college campus missionaries. Why should we give our money for college evangelism when our money can be better utilized to help the young learn Christianity, precluding the need to deal with humanistic, nihilistic, and lost students stepping on to college campuses each fall?

I tried reaching the Christian Establishment for years. The newcomers to this issue look at what I do and wonder, *Why don't we all work together?* I wonder the same thing, and I *would* work with the Christian Establishment if they returned a phone call and then were open to debating these things. But someone like me trying to work with the Christian Establishment is like a conservative trying to work with the Republican Establishment. It is not me who is unwilling; it is them. Hundreds of times I have knocked; there has been no answer.

Throughout this book I have mentioned how increasing private education and decreasing civil government education are two sides of the same coin. That is the case because there is only so much money to go around, meaning some people may want to be involved with furthering private education but they cannot, as the civil government school system has their money. The humanists have the same problem: they want to increase civil government school system size, but the voters (in various ways) reject them as there is no political will for the humanists. It is a zero sum, these competing systems.

Some retort that there is plenty of money to fund both systems, and that Christians who pay property taxes that fund civil government schools could still afford to help increase private education. That is missing the point, as the civil government schools still have some of our money. If we had it back we would be able to better help our aging parents, increase private health care endeavors, feed the homeless, or just invest the money so that society benefits from wealth creation.

When the Establishment preacher suggests we cannot change society by what I do, he imports his misunderstanding of the Mosaic Law (and other parts of Scripture). Law, for example, was only revealed so as to expose our sin[146], so you should know that I am not trying to change people from the outside in. Rather, I utilize law generally to show people we have sinned by allowing the civil government to disciple our children; I utilize the law to show people the ultimate goal, which is to return education jurisdiction to the family and church. But just as there is interplay between law and gospel, there is interplay between private education and abolition, meaning you may be exposed to law and then be forgiven through gospel; or it may be the case that you further experience the gospel, allowing you to further comport with the law. Analogously the same interplay exists between private education and abolition, meaning you may be exposed to private education and then realize there should not be civil government schools; or it may be the case that you learn there should not be civil government schools and you are convicted to privately educate.

---

[146] 1 Timothy 1:8.

To be honest, when I am out and about and I encounter a home school parent and talk to him or her about what I do, he or she is ecstatic. It is the Christian Establishment, the modern theological "expert," with whom I have trouble. In that respect there comes a time when you realize your *papa* is just a man. Likewise, there *should* come a time when you realize your *president* is just a man and your *preacher* is just a man. They are all fallible men. If a papa, preacher, or president mandates you do something that goes against Christianity, you should disobey, to the degree you are able. *I openly encourage a child to disobey his papa, preacher, and president if sent to a civil government school; he or she will be in obedience to God.*

Papas, preachers, and presidents must not be considered elite, infallible humans. You have access to the same information as any Christian Establishment member. We have had Christian Establishments before; and, before, they have been busted—by other Christians. In that regard I put the Christian Establishment on notice. Because of your civil government school system disengagement, you have brought curses down on us. So one of two things is going to happen: either those curses will cause your Establishment to die a slow theological death, or the truth that the Bible does not justify the existence of the civil government school system will cause your Establishment to die a slow theological death. So you can either defeat, retreat, and repeat, or you can repent.

SCRIPTURE INDEX

| 49:1 | 150 |

Jeremiah

| 1:5 | 150 |
| 17:10 | 33 |

Matthew

4:4	18n
5:17	147n
5:27-28	71
9:4	33
12:50	34n
16:19	32n
18:15-17	31n
19:3-9	22n
19:18	151
22:21	139n
22:37	188
23:23	149
23:23-24	146
24:36	155
28:19-20	31n

Luke

2:51	61
10:26	9n
19:13	160n

John

1:3	52n
3:8	70n
4:1-26	11n
18:11	45n

ABOLITION
Overcoming the Christian Establishment on Education

SUBJECT INDEX

ABOLITION
Overcoming the Christian Establishment on Education

Made in the USA
Coppell, TX
22 October 2022

85135373R00142